×Leckie

HIGHER
History

grade **booster**

✕ John A Kerr ✕

Text © 2006 John Kerr
Design and layout © 2006 Leckie & Leckie Ltd
Cover image © Picture Crew/Getty Images

02/060707

ISBN 978-1-84372-376-9

Published by
Leckie & Leckie Ltd, 3rd floor, 4 Queen Street, Edinburgh, EH2 1JE
tel: 0131 220 6831 fax: 0131 225 9987
enquiries@leckieandleckie.co.uk   www.leckieandleckie.co.uk

Special thanks to
Alison Summers (content review), Pumpkin House (illustration), BRW (design and page
make-up), Roda Morrison (copy-editing), Angela Wigmore (proofreading)
and Caleb Rutherford (cover design).

A CIP Catalogue record for this book is available from the British Library.

Leckie & Leckie Ltd is a division of Huveaux plc.

Acknowledgements
Leckie & Leckie has made every effort to trace all copyright holders. If any have been
inadvertently overlooked, we will be pleased to make the necessary arrangements.

We would like to thank the following for permission to reproduce their material:
• Corbis Images/Bettman for the photograph on p 54
• *The Scotsman* Publications Ltd. for an extract from *The Scotsman*, 1 October 1938 (p 70)
• Saqi Books, London, for an extract from A Maalouf,
The Crusades Through Arab Eyes (1983) (p 79)
• News International Newspapers for the cartoon on p 84
• Solo Syndication/Associated Newspapers and Llyfrgell Genedlaethol Cymru/The National
Library of Wales for the cartoon by Illingworth on p 87
• Philip Allan Updates for the extract on p 105

Leckie & Leckie would like to thank the following for permission to reproduce their
copyright material without charge:
• People's Press Printing Society for an extract from *Daily Worker*, 12 March 1938 (p 60)
• Birlinn Ltd. for an extract from W Hamish Fraser and RJ Morris (eds), *People and Society
in Scotland* Vol.II, 1830–1914 (1990). (p 68)
• DCT Syndication for an extract from *Dundee Courier and Advertiser*, 9 March 1936 (p 75)
• Pearson Education Ltd. for an extract from RJ Overy, *The Origins of the Second World
War*, Seminar Studies in History (1987, 1998) (p 105)

CONTENTS

For Hugh Douds, who first set me on this path.

Introduction

Why do I need this book?

How should I use this book?

Must I try to answer all the question examples?

Coursework assessment and the final exam

How do I know I can trust the information in this book?

What will I learn from this book?

Will this book tell me all the facts I need for the exam?

What's in this book?

Is this book of use to me?

WHY DO I NEED THIS BOOK?

Unless you are a guaranteed A pass student – and who is? – this book will help you gain the best possible grades in your Higher History examination.

HOW SHOULD I USE THIS BOOK?

The short answer is you should use the book when you need it!

This book is NOT meant to be read all at once. In fact, some sections may be scary if they deal with parts of the course you have

not yet started. But when you are working on the extended essay, or on how to write essays, or on how to prepare paper 2 answers, or on any other aspect of your Higher History exam, then turn to the relevant section and use it to your advantage.

MUST I TRY TO ANSWER ALL THE QUESTION EXAMPLES?

No. Most students learn about Later Modern history (option C) but some study earlier options (Medieval or Early Modern). This book contains examples from the most popular topics in the Higher History syllabus. Find those that apply to your course of study. However, the skills and techniques for answering questions and writing essays which are fully explained in this book will benefit everyone sitting Higher History, no matter which topics are being studied.

COURSEWORK ASSESSMENT AND THE FINAL EXAM

Higher History coursework comprises three units, all of which involve internal assessments called unit assessments. The following table sets out the unit assessment requirements of Higher History.

Unit assessments

Unit number	Title	Internal assessment
Unit 1	Scottish and British	Units 1 and 2 – one hour essay from a choice of two for each unit. Pass / Fail
Unit 2	European and World	
Unit 3	Historical special topic	Unit 3 – special topic 5 sources and 5 questions to be completed in 85 minutes. Pass / Fail

The examination

Exam title	Task	Time
Extended essay	Issue chosen from syllabus of units 1–3 200 word plan Externally marked 30 marks	2 hours to write up
Paper 1	Two essays, each worth 25 marks One each from units 1 and 2 Total 50 marks	80 minutes
Paper 2	5 source based questions valued between 4 and 8 marks Total 30 marks	85 minutes

HOW DO I KNOW I CAN TRUST THE INFORMATION IN THIS BOOK?

The writer is John Kerr. He is a well-known teacher and author of many books preparing students for History exams. John Kerr is also a marker for the Scottish Qualifications Authority (SQA) and is an exam setter at Higher level. Finally, he also writes the annual 'revision guides' published in the national press each year. So you can trust his advice!

WHAT WILL I LEARN FROM THIS BOOK?

You will learn how to achieve the best possible grades at Higher level. You will learn how to answer the different types of question you will be asked in your exam and for your unit assessments. You will find lots of advice and examples of answers – both good and bad – so that you can improve your own skills.

WILL THIS BOOK TELL ME ALL THE FACTS I NEED FOR THE EXAM?

This book will NOT tell you all the information you need for your Higher History course. All that can be found in two other books from Leckie and Leckie called *Intermediate and Higher History Course Notes*, Books 1 and 2. They are also written by John Kerr.

WHAT'S IN THIS BOOK?

An introductory section provides general advice about your exam.

Chapter 1 focuses on the extended essay. You will write an extended essay weeks before the main exam so this chapter will give you the best possible start towards gaining a very good grade at Higher History.

Chapter 2 focuses on Higher paper 1 in which you will be asked to write two essays. The chapter is divided into sections on writing introductions, developing your essay and reaching – and writing – conclusions. There is also advice about how your essays will be marked.

Chapter 3 explains how to develop the different skills you need to deal with the five different types of questions you will be asked in Higher paper 2. These are:

The evaluation of evidence question

The evaluation of opinion question

The evaluation of a visual source question

The comparison of sources question

The 'big issue' or '8 mark' question.

IS THIS BOOK OF USE TO ME?

Yes! Each section will use examples of questions drawn from the most popular of the Higher History options.

Most question / answer examples will be relevant to Paper 1 Later Modern and Paper 2 special topics 6–9 because these are the most popular choices. But some will come from the earlier sections within the Higher History examination.

And the advice, tips and skills explained in this book apply to everyone!

1 The Extended Essay

Introduction

Choosing my essay title

Planning my essay

Writing my essay

Exam example

INTRODUCTION

At some point in your Higher course you will be asked to write an extended essay. This usually takes place in the spring, about two or three months before the final exam. You will know the title of the essay. You will know how you will construct the essay. You will have a plan guiding what you will write. You will have lots of time. You can't go wrong!

Why is the extended essay important to me?

It is really important to do as well as you can in the extended essay since the mark you get is part of your final Higher exam award total. In fact, the extended essay counts for 30 marks out of a total of 110 – so doing well in the extended essay can provide you with a very useful launch pad for future success. The average mark for extended essays is just over 18 out of 30 – and that's a B! And that's an average. You can achieve more than that.

What is the extended essay?

The extended essay is no different from any other essay – just longer. To sum up in the words of the SQA, the extended essay is a *'top of the range version of what a candidate is capable of given research and writing time'*.

Your teachers and the SQA know that you are unlikely to show off your best possible work in an exam that only allows you 40 minutes to write an essay. That is why the extended essay was introduced. By choosing your own title, having time to research and prepare, and then two hours to write up your essay, you have a chance to create a top of the range essay which shows off the best you can do.

How long does my essay have to be?

The answer is simple – what you can write in two hours! There are NO word limits in the extended essay. Most people can write one page of A4 in ten minutes. Since there are 12 x 10 minutes in two hours then it is possible to write a twelve-page essay and many people do. The bulk of essays are about seven or eight pages long. Certainly, very short essays start alarm bells ringing in the heads of markers given that students have had time to prepare and practise, but each essay is read and marked on its merits.

CHOOSING MY ESSAY TITLE

Should I try to choose a title that is fresh and new and different?

No, it's not necessary and such a choice of essay title could cause you problems. Some candidates disadvantage themselves by selecting inappropriate titles for their essay. Ask your teacher or tutor if you are unsure.

Are there any rules about the title that I can choose?

Yes, there are two main rules.

1 It must be part of the syllabus you are studying. So an essay about the military campaigns of World War Two would risk gaining 0 marks since it is not within any Higher syllabus. Your essay title MUST be part of the Higher History syllabus, checkable at http://www.sqa.org.uk.

2 Your essay title must be issue based and not simply descriptive. In other words there must be an issue or question within your title such as 'Why did America lose the Vietnam War?' or 'How successful was the Labour Government 1945–1951 in dealing with the social problems facing Britain after World War Two?'

A good way to check if your essay is issue based is to look for the question mark at the end of the title. If there is one then your essay should be OK as it will hopefully answer this question.

But if your essay has no question mark at the end – such as 'Appeasement' or 'The Crusades Fail' or 'The Tsar, 1917' or 'Bismarck and the Unification of Germany' – then you are likely to fail. That's because the marker has no way of knowing what you are trying to do apart from write a description of the subject in the title.

Are there types of questions to avoid?

Yes! Weaknesses are most often displayed in certain types of questions. These fall into one or more of several categories. For example:

Double issues

Avoid asking two questions for the price of one. Why give yourself extra work? Bad questions could be:

- **'What problems faced the National Government in 1931 and how successful was it in dealing with them?'**

  OR

- **'Why did the Liberal reforms happen and how successful were they?'**

As a rough guide, avoid the word 'AND' in your questions.

Questions phrased in ways that make their meanings unclear or that lack focus

Sometimes your title can make it hard for a marker to know what you are trying to argue, such as:

- **'Was Rowntree the nagging conscience of the Liberals?'** (The candidate wanted to answer **'Why did the Liberal reforms happen?'**)

  OR

- **'Was Lenin the cork bobbing on the tide of revolution or was he the driving force behind the wave?'** (A better alternative title would be 'How important was Lenin to the Russian Revolution of November 1917?')

What types of questions are good styles to choose?

Please notice that this heading contains the word STYLES. The following are examples of styles of questions which you could adapt to fit in with your preference for a topic. Look at past papers. There is no reason why you can't choose a past paper question. That way you know the question is acceptable to the SQA!

Option A: Medieval

How important were towns to medieval England and Scotland?

Why was Philip II successful in expanding the power of the French monarchy?

How far do you agree that the decline of serfdom in the fourteenth century can be attributed to the Black Death?

Option B: Early Modern

To what extent did Scottish society change between 1542 and 1603?

How important was religion as a cause of unrest in Scotland and England in the reign of Charles I?

How successful were the enlightened reforms of Joseph II?

Option C: Later Modern

To what extent did the Liberal reforms improve the lives of the British people?

How important was Prussian military strength in the unification of Germany by 1871?

Why did the civil rights movement gain so much support in the USA in the 1950s and early 1960s?

Can I write an essay based on my paper 2 special topic?

Yes, you can. But remember there might be some disadvantages. You will not have any past essay titles to give you ideas to choose from. Also, since there is no essay question in paper 2 you will not have the chance of being lucky and seeing your extended essay title cropping up in the final exam.

What if my extended essay title appears in the final exam?

You just got lucky! If you choose your extended essay from 'mainstream titles' it is quite possible your topic, and perhaps even a title similar to your extended essay, will appear in the final exam. There is NO restriction about answering that question using the memory you have of doing the extended essay. But be careful to adapt your information to fit the exact question asked in the exam.

Can I do the same title as my friend?

Yes, you can, but before you do, think carefully.

Is your whole class doing the same title? That might not be a good idea. The SQA is concerned about lots of essays coming from the same centres with the same titles. Such patterns can result from students choosing a title that has been the subject of a class lesson on planning an essay. That approach can help weaker candidates gain confidence by providing a structure to their essay but if you have ambitions to do well then it is always best to do your own work, based of course on advice from your teachers and your experience from doing earlier essays.

PLANNING MY ESSAY

What is the extended essay plan?

Your plan provides a framework for your essay. It demonstrates skills of research, selection and organisation of information, reflection on your work and, finally, reaching a decision about the issue within your title. Your extended essay plan MUST be sent to the SQA with your finished essay, preferably on the official form downloadable from the SQA website at **http://www.sqa.org.uk**. The main point of doing that is to include a word count in the box provided. However, your plan can be spread over as many pages as you like if it helps you. Just attach it to the official form.

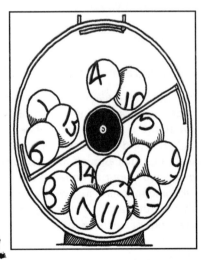

Is the plan really a plan?

It depends on you. Most candidates write out their essay several times before the final 'write up session'. That gives them time to draft their essay and make alterations to the plan. It might also allow teachers and tutors to look over the plan to offer advice although they are not obliged to do so. In such cases your 'plan' is really more of a summary of your essay which will help to remind you of its 'flow' when you write it finally under exam conditions.

On the other hand some candidates make notes and plan out their essay but have not yet fully written it. Either way, make sure your 'plan' assists you to write the best possible essay you can manage.

Will my plan be marked?

The plan is NOT marked but is a vital part of your essay both for your use and for markers to see that you have completed the required planning stage. Nor is there any time limit to a plan. The plan is YOURS. You can change it, colour it or print it out. You can write it anywhere, anytime before you write your extended essay under exam conditions.

Are there any rules about the plan?

Yes, there is one absolute rule. The SQA reported, *'Centres should remind candidates of the 200 word limit for the Extended Essay'*. So your plan must NOT be longer than 200 words. You WILL have marks deducted from your final essay mark if you go over that limit. In years gone by there was some flexibility about going over the word limit. In recent years that has changed. Don't take the chance.

Are diagrams and pictures allowed in the plan?

No. The SQA are aware of some people trying to get round the rules by using code words or pictograms. The SQA's position on this is clear. *'Pictograms, maps, codes and text language will be penalised'*. If it is felt that candidates are trying to 'get round' the rules of the extended essay they will lose marks. However, diagrams such as mind maps are acceptable. The SQA guidance states, *'mind maps and colour to enhance the organisation of the plan are permissible'*. After all, mind maps are just words organised with boxes and lines and colour around them. But ways of increasing the number of words, such as using small drawings or cartoons in the plan are dealt with seriously – and watch out for the words you write on your mind map. They are also counted as part of your 200 words.

Can I use abbreviations?

Yes, but what's the point? Each abbreviation will still be counted as a word so abbreviations will not reduce the total number of words!

How should I write and use my plan?

Your plan should be exactly that – a plan of the essay you will write. Your plan should NOT be just a collection of facts, figures and quotes. It is NOT a random selection of research notes. It is a PLAN!

Even if your essay was lost somehow a marker should be able to see what your essay structure would be, the main ideas you would include, the sequence of your essay and how you would structure your essay – all just by looking at your plan. After all, your plan is meant to help you by reminding you what should be in your essay.

A few people write their essay 'fresh' in the exam room, using their plan as a help. That means they have not written the essay before. I don't recommend that.

Most people have written their extended essay several times before they write the real extended essay in the exam. By doing that you have several advantages. First of all you allow yourself a chance to rethink and edit your work. It is your choice if you word process or handwrite at this stage. Word processed work is easier to change by cutting and pasting, spell checking and so on. But handwriting is practice for the time you will have in the exam and also, by rewriting over again, you will establish your essay in your memory.

Secondly, once your draft has been written you may be lucky enough to have a teacher or tutor who will read over your essay and make suggestions for improvement.

Finally, when you have rewritten the essay two or three times you will have a fairly clear idea of what you will write and how long it will take you. Now you must distil the essay into a 200 word plan.

How should I organise my plan?

Since your introduction is vital for reasons outlined below (page 21) you could have your introduction written out in condensed form but as close to the real thing as possible. You could use about 60–70 words for this. Your outline introduction could also have your main ideas and themes which you will develop later. Even the SQA recommends an approach like this by writing, *'Many candidates merely produce a "story" in the extended essay. An analytical approach assisted by the use of a clear plan to provide a clear structure to the essay would have assisted such "average" candidates.'*

Moving on to the main body of your essay, you could aim to write a series of key sentences that would start off each paragraph – although a well-written introduction should signpost what each paragraph should be about.

If you are intending to write about eight paragraphs, each one in your plan should be allocated ten words. That means you will use about 80 words.

Remember you should use supporting evidence throughout your essay. History skills should run through the essay so that means you must not only use factual detail, but also be prepared to use quotes and make reference if you can to the reliability and accuracy of the information used. If you are using quotes do not waste words copying them out fully in your plan. Each quote should be boiled down to essential words to prompt you.

It is also helpful to remind yourself to include mini conclusions linking each paragraph back to the main title so you keep your arguments going and don't fall back into storytelling with little connection to the main question.

Finally you must have a strong conclusion. It is really important to summarise your main ideas and prioritise your information to arrive at a direct, balanced answer to the main question. You might want to write out the skeleton of your conclusion and if you have followed the word allocation so far you will have at least 50 words for this. That's about six lines of normal writing! So you could really work on your conclusion and have most of it in your plan. And remember – try to ensure your conclusion ends on a high note, perhaps with an appropriate quote that provides an overall answer to the question or which supports your main argument.

Is there anything else I can do to prepare effectively?

The layout of your plan can be made to work for you. Empty space is free so use it to lay out the plan clearly for you to see what is going where, and in what order.

What does a weak and a better essay plan look like?

This first plan is based around the title **'Why did Robert the Bruce succeed in gaining Scottish independence where others had failed?'**

PLAN (If your plan exceeds 200 words in length you may lose up to 10 marks)

WALLACE

STRONG BRIDGE
GUARDIANSHIP NOT NOBLE – NO SUPPORT
FALKIRK ESCAPED ABROAD
GUERILLA WARFARE
DIPLOMACY

ENGLISH WEAKNESS

WARS ON 3 FRONTS: SCOTLAND, FRANCE + WALES

CHURCH / DIPLOMACY

DECLARATION OF THE CLERGY 1309 – ACKNOWLEDGEMENT OF BRUCE, DENOUNCED
BALLIOL
DECLARATION OF ARBROATH 1320 LETTER TO POPE
SUPPORTED WALLACE + BRUCE

UNCONQUERABLE SCOTLAND

GEOGRAPHICALLY UNCONTROLLABLE DUE TO MOUNTAINS, HILLS ETC
SMALL COMMUNITIES

ROBERT BRUCE

BANNOCKBURN
RAIDS TO NORTHERN ENGLAND
ROXBURGH
SCOTTISH INDEPENDENCE / TREATY OF NORTHAMPTON 1328
ST ANDREWS

CONCLUSION

ROUND UP ALL SECTIONS EVENLY + COME TO BALANCED CONCLUSION

Why is this a weak plan?

The plan on the previous page is too short. You are allowed 200 words, so why not use them all to your advantage? This plan is only about 90 words.

There are at least some headings but the plan is mainly a list of facts, names and events. There is no reminder about ideas or the argument which is implicit in the title.

Remember, your essay is about an issue which will be debated. That means different points of view should be included and there should be a theme or argument running through your essay supporting your ideas. In this case, what were the reasons why Bruce succeeded where others failed? There are no suggestions of reasons in this plan.

The real indication of just how weak this essay plan is lies in the conclusion: introductions and conclusions are vital in an essay. This plan has neither. It goes straight into a catalogue of facts, suggesting that this candidate has just not thought through what should be in the essay. Essentially the plan for the conclusion translates as 'Write a conclusion' – not a very helpful plan!

The next plan is better. It is based around the title **'Assess the contribution of Bismarck to the unification of Germany'**.

PLAN (If your plan exceeds 200 words in length you may lose up to 10 marks)

Intro
- He was main factor
- Strength of Prussian Military
- Prussia's economic success
- Unity of Germany

Germany's
Previous
State
- Thirty-Nine separate states with common identities
- The Bund and the Zollverein
- German Confederation and free trade area
- Common features of culture and speech

French
Revolution
- Napoleon takes over Europe with ease
- Fears for defence measures of German states
- Frankfurt Parliament 1848 dominated by Prussia
- Outlined needs for military and leader
- Released the concepts of liberty, equality and fraternity

Germany
Divided
- Two main states: Prussia and Austria
- Austria has arch opponents of nationalism, was an Empire
- Prussia promoted industrialisation, wanted to lead unification, wanted Austria out of unification, Kleindeutsch

Bismarck
- Who was he?
- Chancellor after the Military crisis
- His beliefs and aims
- Influence gained over foreign affairs

Bismarck's
Movement
- Gaining of Schleswig and Holstein
- Start of Austrian war – cunning and manipulative
- Never destroyed Austria
- Why France was a threat
- How he overcame it
- Results from three wars
- Where and why German Empire was declared

Conclusion
- Explain mini-factors of unification
- Explain why these mattered
- Bismarck was main factor
- How he achieved his aims

Why is this a better (but not great!) plan?

The answer should already be clear to you. It uses most of the word allocation – about 180 words. There is a structure – introduction, development and conclusion. There are facts but also ideas which will further the argument such as 'releasing concepts of liberty, equality and fraternity'. There is a conclusion which sums up the main argument outlined in the introduction.

But watch out – this is an acceptable plan but it's not the best. There are no reminders of historiography. The introduction is still weak with many important issues relevant to German unification left out. However, there is enough here to remind the writer of the essay of the main points and if the points are developed well the candidate should get into the B range of marks.

Finally, a word about language and style. The SQA gives explicit advice. *'Candidates should not use informal casual style such as "In this essay I hope to ..." or "In my conclusion I have shown that ...". At Higher level a more formal and mature style of writing is expected.'* In other words avoid using 'I' or phrases such as 'I think' or 'I will explain'. DO NOT USE the first person. Try to write in a clear and adult style avoiding slang terms, vague generalisations or text language.

WRITING MY ESSAY

How should I write my essay?

In recent years markers at the SQA have noticed big improvements in essay structures, with much better uses of introductions and conclusions. Poorer candidates still rely on 'In this essay I will' or 'This essay will look at' or 'In order to answer this question we must answer' but most candidates avoid these clichés. They know that to be successful essays MUST have a recognisable structure which means there must be an introduction, a middle section developing the ideas of the introduction and a conclusion. There is much more advice on essay structure in the next chapter dealing with Paper 1.

Must I include lots of quotes from historians?

The SQA recently reported *'Many candidates showed good knowledge and understanding of historical content and in some cases there was also evidence of awareness of historical debate and the use of historiography.'* It continued, *'There are signs of some candidates developing a number of skills including research into a variety of sources, awareness of historical debate and historiography, with selective and constructive use of quotations from historical sources. All of these contributed to well-structured essays.'*

Do I need to know what *historiography* is?

Yes. History is about researching and explaining the past and that is what historians do. Historiography is the study of historians and what they wrote. Often historians have different opinions so by using your knowledge of these differing opinions you will be able to make a more effective debate type answer. Including quotes to support your ideas can also help and remember to credit those quotes with the author's name.

But beware! Avoid using trivial 'quotes' to create a bogus impression of real research. For example, one candidate wrote, 'World War broke out in 1914 (AJP Taylor)'. Any quotes you use should express the point of view of the author and if possible be contrasted with a differing point of another source. One word of warning – 'invented' quotes are usually extremely obvious. They are easily spotted and punished!

So to summarise, if your essay takes an issue and looks at different viewpoints and differing interpretations of what happened and why it happened, then you are likely to do well.

Must I include quotes to get an A award?

It is NOT TRUE to think an A grade award is impossible without quotes from named historians. Every year many candidates get A awards because they use information accurately and relevantly to argue their cases without a historian's name in sight!

What makes a good extended essay structure?

There is not much difference between an extended essay and a normal class essay. By the time you do your extended essay you should know that essay writing is not just about facts but also about a structured argument. To find out more about essay structure look at the section in this book on essay writing skills (pages 30–46). But there are points about the extended essay worth mentioning here.

Your introduction is the most vital part of any essay

Your introduction creates a first impression and it gets a marker on your side if you show that you are arguing a case, not just telling a story. Your introduction should provide a clear indication of the route you intend to take through your essay and your introductory points must be developed through the rest of your essay. Once you have a good introduction the rest of the essay should flow logically from it. You should be able to use your introduction as a point by point paragraph guide. This introduction to an essay on the growth of democracy shows what I mean.

EXAM EXAMPLE

Did Britain become more democratic between 1850 and 1918?

For any country to be called democratic certain conditions have to exist. First of all adults should have the vote **(1)** but the right to vote itself did not make Britain democratic. Between 1850 and 1918 other features in a democracy were created. These features included a fair system of voting **(2)**, a choice of who to vote for **(3)** and access to information to make an informed choice. **(4)** It should also be possible for adults to become MPs themselves **(5)** and parliament should be accountable to the voters **(6)**. Between 1850 and 1918 most, but not all, of these conditions had been met so Britain was more of a democracy but not entirely democratic.

You'll see there are six numbered points. When you write your own introductions, it's a good tip to number faintly your main ideas – that tells you how many separate middle section paragraphs there should be to develop.

Middle section

The long middle section of your essay must develop each one of the themes, points or issues raised in your introduction.

Each new point should be a new paragraph. Each new paragraph must start with a key sentence that makes clear what the point of the paragraph will be. At the end of each paragraph try to link the point you have developed to the main question. That sentence shows to a marker that your paragraph is relevant to the overall title and that you are answering the question.

After one well-structured paragraph go on to the next. It should be based on the next point raised in your introduction. Keep following the same format advice, continuing your main argument and showing off more of your factual knowledge. Continue in the same way until, you have completed all your paragraphs.

The conclusion

Your conclusion must weigh up your evidence and lead to an overall answer to the title question. You should prioritise the reasons that support your answer which means you should make clear which parts of your answer are more important than others. You should also deal with evidence or opinions with which you do not agree and explain why you do not agree with them. What criticisms can you make of the evidence?

It's often useful to finish with a quote that sums up your view, but don't repeat one already used.

As a final check make sure you have made clear your answer to the big question asked in the essay title.

And finally ...

You should now be ready to tackle your extended essay. Good luck! But remember that people make their own luck and success in the extended essay comes from careful preparation and then putting your preparation into practice by using the two hours to show off your best possible work.

2 Higher History Paper 1

INTRODUCTION

When you get your exam booklet it might look worryingly large. Do not worry. The booklet contains sections on all three options. You only have to deal with one of those options.

What are the three options?

The three options are called:

- A   Medieval
- B   Early Modern
- C   Later Modern

Within each option there are two Historical Studies. One is called Scottish and British. The other is called European and the World.

Do I have to choose which option to answer?

No. Your teacher / tutor will have made the decision which option you study. You have only studied one option. Most schools and colleges teach the Later Modern period.

RACE AGAINST TIME – PAPER 1

What do I have to do?

Your Higher History paper 1 will contain the following instructions:

> Answer TWO questions, one from Historical Study: Scottish and British and one from Historical Study: European and the World.

> The Scottish and British historical study section will give you a choice of five questions from which you choose ONE question to answer.

> The European and the World section will give you a choice of four questions from which you must choose ONE to answer.

> The answers to the questions must be written in the form of essays.

How much time do I have to complete paper 1?

The paper 1 examination lasts for 1 hour 20 minutes (80 minutes).

Your target is to write TWO essays in 80 minutes.

Should I do two essays from the same section if I don't see any questions I want to answer in the other section?

No. Never do two essays from the same historical study. If you do, both essays will be marked but only the essay with the best mark will be counted. The other essay will get 0 marks, no matter how good it is.

If I spend too long on the first essay should I still try to do a second essay?

Yes! First of all DO NOT spend too long on one essay. You MUST be disciplined about time and spend only 40 minutes on your first essay. Otherwise, any time taken over 40 minutes is really time being stolen from your second essay.

If you are overrunning time it means you have not really planned out your strategy and are relying on cramming in more and more information. You are unlikely to be heading towards a good mark. Even if it is a good essay you might get 16 marks after 40 minutes and by spending more time you might push it into A pass range and get 20. (That's unlikely, but stick with this example.) That means you have gained 4 marks by overshooting time. Unless your second essay is completely and utterly wrong, irrelevant or only lasts a few lines you are guaranteed to get more than 4 marks. If your second essay even slightly tries to answer the question – even if there are errors and some of it is irrelevant – you will still get about 8 or 9 marks. So, with the example here, 16 marks plus 9 equals 25 marks – and that's a pass since 25 / 50 is half marks.

By sticking with one essay, even one which is a good A pass you will only get 20 / 50 – a poor fail.

The rule is this: organise your time and do TWO ESSAYS.

THE ESSAY QUESTIONS

What will the essay questions be like?

ALL essays are a similar style. You will never get a 'tell a story' essay which asks you only to 'describe'. In the Higher History exam you will always be asked whether or not you agree with a particular point of view or you will be asked to explain something.

Examples from the Later Modern option

> To what extent did women get the right to vote in 1918 because of their war work?

> 'Fascist domestic policies were a triumph more of propaganda than of genuine achievement'. How acceptable is this view of either Germany 1933 or Italy 1922–1939?

(NB. If you have studied this period you will have learned about Germany or Italy. In the exam you are only expected to write about one of these countries.)

Why did the Bolsheviks win the civil war in Russia?

How far did black radical protest movements achieve their aims by 1969?

Examples from the Early Modern option

Did Mary Queen of Scots deserve to lose her throne?

'Myth rather than reality'. To what extent is this an accurate assessment of the absolutism of Louis XIV?

Explain the decision to abolish the monarchy in 1792 in France.

Examples from the Medieval option

'With the reign of David I the kingship of Scotland moved to a new era'. Discuss.

Is it fair to say that Robert Bruce was more interested in his own gain than in Scottish independence?

Is there a 'must remember' rule about writing essays?

Yes. Answer the question that is asked – not the question you would like to see in the exam paper. The SQA has reported that if candidates carefully read each question and worked out what it asked them to do it would make a massive contribution to raising standards of performance. Every year markers find a significant number of prepared essays that did not directly answer the questions asked in the exam paper. The reason for this is that candidates presumably hoped for different questions and failed to adapt their answers. Don't be one of these candidates.

What should I do when I first look at the essay questions in the exam?

You will be nervous and adrenaline will be pumping. You will want to get started quickly.

The first thing to do is breathe deeply. Then make sure you are looking at the questions in the section of the course you have studied. Then look for questions you might want to answer. Then make sure you have understood not only what the question is about but also what you have to do. In other words, see what the topic is but also what the task is that you have to do.

Finally, read all the questions again and make sure the one you have chosen gives you the best chance to score highly.

Should I write a mini plan for my essay?

Many candidates find it helpful to write a mini plan along the lines of the signpost idea explained later in this chapter (page 31). Briefly, a signpost simply shows where your essay is going. It makes you think about the question and what you need to do to be successful. You then need to think what the main relevant sections to be included should be. Once you have done that you have the main skeleton of your essay planned out. That's your signpost. You can bullet these points at the start of your essay or draw a small spider diagram – whatever helps you get started on an organised, relevant answer to the question.

How do I make sure I answer the question properly?

The single most important piece of advice to any candidate is 'read the question: what does it ask you to do?'

Any essay question has two parts – the TOPIC and the TASK. The topic is what you will see first when you open your exam paper and look at the questions quickly. You will be asking yourself what the essays are about. Do you know information about this topic? The task is to understand what you have to DO with your information. Are you sure you understand what the question wants you to do? How do you make your information RELEVANT to the answer?

Candidates who score highly in paper 1 do so because they read the question and then answer the question asked, not the one they practised weeks or months before.

Is it enough just to write out as much information as I know?

No, it is not. Essay writing is about knowing detailed information BUT it is even more important to know the process and technique of HOW to write a good essay. An essay is not just a long story putting in as many names, dates and facts as you can. Your answer must be relevant to the question. It must also be structured with a beginning, middle and an end.

Why must I have a structure to my essays?

If you don't know where you are going you will never get there. In other words, a successful essay needs a plan. That plan must help you answer the question set. You will never get a question that states, 'Write all you know about ....'. You will be asked to use information and your own thoughts to argue your case.

You could be asked whether you agree with an opinion or not.

You might be asked to explain why certain things happened.

You might be asked to judge if something was a success or failure.

All these types of questions require you to answer in a thoughtful, structured way.

WRITING AN INTRODUCTION

Why is an introduction important?

An introduction is where your essay starts to take life – or starts to struggle. Without an introduction there will be no structure because you have not thought HOW you intend to answer the question.

If your plan is not sorted out before you write your introduction, your essay will decline into storytelling – at best a C award. The introduction is where you must do your hardest thinking about the topic and the task and what will be the main stages of your answer.

Your introduction should signpost your main ideas. It should provide you with a sequenced guide to follow through the rest of the essay.

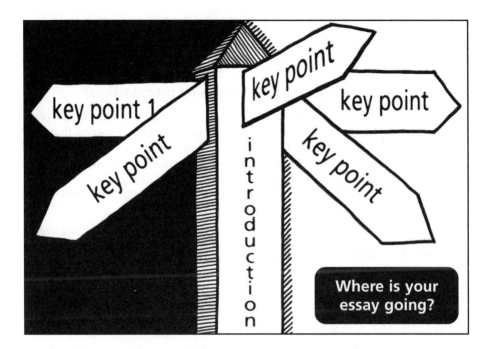

What is the first thing I should do before I write my introduction?

The first thing to do is to make sure you are answering the question that is asked, not what you think it might mean on first glance.

Suppose the first question you look at is this:

> How far was concern over poverty a main cause of the Liberal reforms from 1906?

First of all THINK! And ask yourself what the question is about. At first you will see the words 'Liberal', 'reform' and '1906' – it looks like it is about the Liberal reforms. But it is not.

The essay title provides one possible explanation of why the Liberal reforms happened and you are asked if you agree with that view or should other reasons be considered. So the question is really about WHY the Liberal reforms happened. You have to decide if concern over poverty was the real reason why the Liberal reforms happened or if other reasons were more important.

You should know there were other reasons apart from concern over poverty. This question asks 'How far was' so you should be aware that you must show off your knowledge about the other reasons and arrive eventually at a balanced conclusion.

Are there certain things that must be in an introduction?

Yes, it must have a sentence which suggests you are going to write a balanced essay by looking at all sides of the debate. You could do that by stating that concern over poverty was only one of many reasons. Then you should mention the other reasons but do not explain them yet. Remember this is your introduction. It should be written in a 'grown up' style avoiding the first person as in 'I think ...', and try to avoid just listing your main points.

What is the difference between a poor introduction and a good one?

To answer that question it is best to use some real examples.

EXAM EXAMPLE 1

This is a very weak introduction.

In order to answer this question it is necessary to explain why the Liberal reforms happened and decide if concern over poverty was a main reason. The Liberal Reforms began in 1906 and were passed to help the old, the young, the sick and the unemployed.

Why is this a very weak introduction?

It is far too short – only two sentences long. This introduction does nothing to help the writer. Time is wasted by almost writing out the question. All it does is pretend to be an introduction. There is no thought here about how the essay will develop. There is no signposting of any ideas about why the reforms happened. The second sentence is completely irrelevant by writing about the reforms, suggesting the writer has not understood the question.

Here is a better, but still not very good introduction.

There were many reasons why the Liberal reforms were passed after 1906 and concern over poverty was one reason. Reports on poverty from Rowntree and Booth were important. Rowntree was a York businessman and Booth was a London one and they both found out that almost 30% of the population in their cities lived in poverty. The Liberals were also worried about national efficiency and national security. There were also new ideas about what the Liberal Party should do to help people too poor to help themselves.

Why is this better but not very good?

The writer understands that the question is about why the reforms were passed but the reasons are listed in a very basic way. There is also extra information developing the point about poverty reports which is not appropriate in an introduction. Detailed information is not needed in an introduction. However, this introduction does provide a foundation to build on.

Here is a much better introduction.

> By the early 20th century most men, rich and poor, could vote. The new Labour Party promised social reform and the Liberals were worried about losing votes. A way had to found of keeping the working class votes. **(1)** Reform could therefore be seen as a rather selfish, political advantageous response to political change rather than simply a response to concern about the poor, highlighted by the reports of Booth and Rowntree which argued that 1/3 of Britain's population lived in poverty. **(2)** Other factors also played a part. The Liberals were concerned that Britain was losing its status as a major industrial and military power while concern over national efficiency and security played a part in the reforms. **(3/4)** Finally new attitudes in the Liberal Party, called New Liberalism, caused the Liberals to move away from the laissez faire ideology of the 19th century. **(5)**

Why is this a better introduction?

It is an appropriate length. The style is mature and signposts clearly the points to be raised in the essay.

If it helps, there is no reason why you cannot faintly number your separate points with a pencil as a guide to yourself what the main development paragraphs should be about.

It provides a structure which the candidate can follow through the rest of the exam.

There is no irrelevance and it is clear to a marker you have understood the question.

Here is another reminder about introduction techniques, this time from a question on German nationalism. The question this time is:

> **How valid was Bismarck's opinion that the period from 1815–1848 was a time when nothing happened?**

First of all remember the importance of identifying both topic and task!

Decide what the question is about **(the topic)** – and be careful! Although the question mentions Bismarck, this essay is NOT about him. It's about developments in German nationalism between 1815 and 1848.

Decide what you have to do **(the task)**. The question is really asking for your ideas about what happened to encourage nationalism between 1815 and 1848.

You have been given one opinion ('a time when nothing happened') and that might refer to political nationalism after the Carlsbad Decrees since it was true that little political change happened between 1815 and 1848.

But you should also know that things such as cultural nationalism, the industrial revolution, the Zollverein and the spread of roads and railways all happened before 1848 so some things were happening. Mention all these points briefly in your introduction. You will explain all these points more fully later.

All you are doing is showing the marker you know what the question means and what direction your essay will take.

DEVELOPING MY ESSAY

Any essay must have a beginning and middle and an end. This section is about the middle part of your essay which will become the longest part of your essay. It is here that you must develop or expand the points made in your introduction. That is why markers and teachers often refer to the middle part as the development section of your essay.

What information should I include in the middle section?

Most of the development section of your essay will contain detailed information but beware you don't wander off into irrelevant storytelling. When you reach the end of a paragraph ask yourself, 'Why have I written this section?' If you don't know why, how will a marker know? Make sure you make your material relevant by ending each paragraph with a mini conclusion linking back to the main question.

Should I try to use primary or secondary evidence in essay development?

Yes, if you can. The opinions of historians, contemporary views or statistics can all be used to support your argument but the important word here is relevance. Do they reinforce points you are making or are you just including such evidence as 'stand alone' with no direct connection to the question set? If there is no connection to the main question then you must think seriously about the inclusion of such material. Although the information you want to include is detailed and accurate, you might lose marks if it is not used in a relevant way within your essay.

What is a good and bad development paragraph?

Here are examples of different development paragraphs from a question from the USA topic.

EXAM EXAMPLE 2

> **Why did the civil rights movement in the USA achieve success in the 1950s and 60s?**

The introduction to this essay had already signposted that one important reason was the gaining of national publicity and that is the point the following paragraphs try to develop.

Here is a weak development paragraph.

In 1955 Rosa Parks sat on a 'whites only' seat in Birmingham Alabama **[That's a factual error. It was Montgomery, Alabama]** and refused to get up when she was asked to. Rosa was tired and was arrested. When news spread about her arrest a bus boycott started and it lasted over a year. There were also sit ins and freedom rides and a March on Washington.

Why is this a weak paragraph?

There is no starting main sentence linking to the introduction that lets a marker know what to expect. There are factual errors. For a good mark your information must be accurate and relevant. This essay wanders into irrelevance by writing too much about Rosa Parks. It is poorly organised, bringing in other protests that are not explained.

There is no clear connection between the information, the point about publicity or even the main question. In other words there is no sign of this information being used to make a point relevant to the main question.

Here is a much better development paragraph.

The gaining of sympathy and publicity by protests was a vital part of the success of the civil rights campaigns. When Rosa Parks refused to give up her seat on a bus in Montgomery Alabama she started a bus boycott which gained wide publicity and led to the emergence of an important leader, Martin Luther King – two vital ingredients in explaining why the campaigns were successful. King's speeches were eventually shown live on national television, proving the importance of the media, especially TV news, for attracting sympathy and support.

Why is this a much better paragraph?

Because it is almost the opposite of the weak one! A strong main sentence links to the introduction and lets a marker know what to expect. There are no factual errors and the information included is relevant to the question. There is no doubt this information is being used to make a point – there is a mini conclusion linking directly to the main question. Throughout the paragraph there are several links back to the main question so the marker is quite clear why the factual information is being included in the essay.

Do I have to write a development paragraph for every main point I put in my introduction – and how do I do it?

Yes, you do, and building a good development paragraph is straightforward once you have a clear introduction.

You might remember from the section on writing introductions that one tip is to remind yourself about the main points in an answer by numbering them in your introduction. That way you have thought out what the main points will be and you have organised the sequence of paragraphs in the development section and decided what they will be about. All you have to do is develop the ideas!

Here is an example from the Later Modern section on Britain and Scotland.

EXAM EXAMPLE 3

> **Why was the right to vote given to more and more people between 1867 and 1918?**

Here is a good introduction to the question.

There were many reasons why the franchise (the right to vote) was extended to more and more people in 1867, 1884 and 1918. **(1)** These reasons included trying to win advantages for a particular political party **(2)**, changing attitudes towards the 'lower classes' **(3)** and the effect of the Great War **(4)** which acted as a catalyst and speeded up change. Probably the most important reason was the effect of the industrial revolution **(5)** that changed where people lived, how they worked and how they felt about their position in society. Finally, another important reason why the franchise was extended was the change in political ideology **(6)** from believing the right to vote should only belong to people who owned the land of Britain to believing that the vote should be the right of all adult British citizens.

Now see the sort of information you would be expected to include in each paragraph to develop it suitably.

(1)   This point sets the context, establishes that you know what the question is about and shows you know when the reform acts were passed. It also lets a marker know that you intend to deal with why the reforms happened (which is what the question asks) rather than write down the terms of the act which is seldom asked about directly.

(2)   This is a reference to political parties adopting the ideas of other parties and attracting voters by promising changes in order to prevent the other party from winning an election. That was especially true of the circumstances around the 1867 Reform Act. The phrases 'stealing the Liberals' clothes' and 'dishing the Whigs' would be appropriate here once you know what they mean!

(3)   Here the point should be made that by 1867 urban skilled working class men were educated and not revolutionary – so why not admit them to the political system by granting them the vote? In 1884 the same was true of other men in the countryside and in towns. If they were not admitted they might turn to the new ideology of socialism which was seen as a threat. There were also views that working people as citizens of the country deserved to have a vote as the ideology of democracy gained greater acceptance in the country. Another more cynical point could be that the ordinary electorate could only vote and had no political influence within parliament. They were far from the reins of power, which were still in the hands of an educated and wealthy elite within parliament.

(4)   The Great War changed many attitudes. Most answers state that women gained the vote because of their war work. That is not entirely true. Most of the women who worked in the war effort were below 30 so they got no vote in 1918. Perhaps there were other reasons for extending the franchise in 1918? One clue could be that for one election only right after the war ex-servicemen who were 19 or over gained the vote. So perhaps changes in the right to vote had more to do with the conscription of young men to fight and the realisation that as citizens, people had the right to choose governments which may decide to send men off to kill on behalf of that government? So maybe this point about the effect of the Great War is not as simple as is first thought. After all, this reform extended the vote to all MEN over 21 as well as women over 30. But the war was certainly a catalyst for change.

(5)   This is an important point to make. Britain was changing very fast after 1850. Cities were growing and social classes were emerging. Large cities and factories housed thousands of people who suffered terrible working and living conditions. If they were not taken 'into' the system by giving them the vote, would they try to overthrow the system with revolution? It was also true that other industrialised countries were becoming more democratic. Political 'freedom' issues had become popular in the USA and Europe in the later 19th century. Why not in Britain also?

(6)   A main theme in this course is change in ideology. By 1918 there was a belief that parliament represented the people of Britain, not just the owners of land and property. A point to make could be that by 1918 the vote was considered to be a right for the many and not a privilege for the few.

To sum up, are there certain things that must be in this middle section?

Yes. Here is a checklist for the essential structure of your middle section:

1. You should have an introductory sentence for each paragraph outlining what the paragraph will be about.
2. You must develop one main point per paragraph.
3. Each paragraph should end with a clear, relevant link back to the main question.
4. Your information must be detailed, accurate and relevant.
5. Your subject specific vocabulary must be very accurate and correctly used. That means that names, ideas and events relevant to the topic must be correctly used.
6. You make regular clear links between the content of each paragraph and the main question.

REACHING AND WRITING CONCLUSIONS

Must I finish with a conclusion?

Your conclusion is as important as all the other sections in your essay. Unless you have a suitable conclusion you are likely to gain less than half marks. Quite simply, you must have a conclusion that ends your essay by summing up your main arguments and providing a final answer to the main question.

What is a suitable conclusion?

A suitable conclusion is a paragraph at the end of your essay that makes clear you are summing up your essay and providing a final overall answer to the question set. It should last about five or six lines of a regular essay and preferably start with words such as 'Finally ...' or 'In conclusion ...'.

Are there rules about what should be in a conclusion?

Yes. You must make your mind up and answer the main question.

You should also sum up your main points. This can be a bit repetitive in that you will be mentioning the main points made in your introduction. To make your conclusion effective and different, try to prioritise your reasons. This means you decide which of the many relevant points you raised in your introduction is the most important in the answer to the main question.

NEVER ever add more factual information into your conclusion. A conclusion ends your essay. It should not continue your essay or push it in a new direction by including new information.

What makes a good conclusion?

EXAM EXAMPLE 4

Suppose you were writing an essay about why the Liberal reforms happened. Earlier in this book you worked on an introduction to the question:

> **How far was concern over poverty a main cause of the Liberal reforms?**

Throughout your essay, you should have been arguing a case and perhaps weighing up different reasons to explain why the Liberal reforms happened. You would explain why concern over poverty was an important reason but you would also have considered other reasons why the reforms happened. In your conclusion you would have to make your mind up and answer the main question. Here are two examples of possible conclusions.

This is a weak conclusion.

The Liberal reforms happened because the politicians were concerned about the poor. Booth and Rowntree proved that people were poor through no fault of their own and the reforms aimed to help the old, the young, the sick and the unemployed.

Why is this a weak conclusion?

It is weak because it does not make clear it is a conclusion. This conclusion makes an unsupported statement that simply states that the reason suggested in the title is true. There is no balance here summing up the other reasons nor any attempt to decide which were the most important reasons. It is also irrelevant to mention the reforms that were later passed. They have no place in an essay on why the reforms happened.

Here is a better conclusion.

In conclusion, the Liberal reforms were a result of many issues. Concern over the poor was one of them. There were also worries about national efficiency and security, new political ideas and winning political advantage over the new Labour Party which had been formed in 1900 and was competing for votes from the working classes who had gained votes in 1884. By 1906 the Liberals were afraid they might lose votes.

Why is this a better conclusion, but not a good one?

It starts by making clear that this is the conclusion. It sums up points that have been developed earlier in the essay. But then it continues to give information that is detailed, new and irrelevant. The creation of the Labour Party was perhaps an influence on the Liberals but details about it certainly should not appear in the conclusion summing up those influences. The place to put that detail is in the appropriate development paragraph earlier in the essay.

Here is a good conclusion.

In conclusion, the Liberal reforms were the result of many influences. Political willingness to pass reforms was influenced by new ideas about state intervention and new Liberalism. Fears of losing votes to the new Labour Party may have made the reforms a more pressing necessity.

Meanwhile, concern about Britain's position in the world made politicians realise that a healthier working class was necessary. However, without the reports of Booth and Rowntree making people aware of dire poverty in Britain perhaps the Liberals would not have responded with a programme of reforms. These reports made people realise that poverty was often beyond the individual's ability to help themselves and the concept of the deserving poor requiring assistance was at the core of the Liberal Reforms.

Why is this a very good conclusion?

This conclusion meets all the requirements of a conclusion. It is clearly marked as the conclusion. It sums up the main issues developed in the essay. At the same time, it prioritises the reasons by suggesting some were much more influential than others. Finally the quality of written English, the vocabulary, the awareness of essay structure and an argued case puts this well into the A pass category.

Now try the same rules about conclusions on an essay from 'The Growth of Nationalism' section – Germany. This example is from the popular and regularly examined section on the role of Bismarck in German unification. Here is the title:

> **'There was nothing inevitable about German unification. Although Bismarck made the most of his chances, he would not have succeeded without good luck.' Do you agree?**

Before you can understand why any conclusion is good or bad, the course of the preceding essay has to be outlined – read this as a piece of revision about essay structure!

First of all remember topic and task! This question is mainly about Bismarck's role in the process of German unification. The first part of the question refers to the argument that unification would have happened anyway, regardless of Bismarck, because of the pressures that were increasing in the 19th century. The second part of the question asks about Bismarck's importance. You must decide how far Bismarck's skills were important, how far he was just lucky and also what other factors were pushing Germany towards unification.

In your introduction you could start by indicating the three sections of this essay. First, outline the developments which laid the foundations of unification before the 1860s such as Prussian economic power, the Zollverein and Austria's declining power. Secondly, outline the importance of Bismarck's diplomacy. Finally, mention that the circumstances outwith Bismarck's control which arose were used by Bismarck to his advantage. In other words, signpost the main directions your essay will take.

In your middle section the bulk of your answer must be on Bismarck – his diplomacy and strategy, his three wars and how he 'Prussianised' the German states. You should also deal with situations and events which cropped up outwith Bismarck's control but which he used to his advantage. Consider their importance. Would Bismarck have been so successful without these events? Or does the importance of these events lie in the way Bismarck used them for his own ends? How far was Bismarck a catalyst? These questions raised are vital to your overall answer. Look back at the title and you will see all of these questions are part of the overall answer.

In your conclusion you must sum up your main points and decide how far Bismarck himself was responsible for German unification. Certainly, without a reformed army, a revived economy, nationalist enthusiasm and several coincidental pieces of luck such as the Hohenzollern Candidature, Bismarck could not have united Germany.

But it's certainly NOT wise to argue that Bismarck was just lucky in the sense of being the right man in the right place at the right time. A suitable ending to your conclusion could be to argue that Bismarck was a catalyst and although he did not control events, he had the ability to use the opportunities they offered.

To illustrate the advice about ending an essay with some impact, think about using either direct quotes or one adapted for your own use – 'in the words of one historian, Bismarck was like a card player who, although he did not deal the cards, played his hand very well.'

MARKING ESSAYS

How will my essay be marked?

When doing any piece of work that is to be assessed or marked it makes a lot of sense to know how it will be marked. That way you can make sure all the things a marker is looking for are included in your essay. This section will help you to organise your essays so that you can get the best marks possible.

What do marks mean?

The first thing to realise is that the marks you get in class will not automatically be the same as you will get awarded by the SQA in the final exam. Teachers and tutors use marking as a teaching tool. Sometimes, early in the course, marking might be a bit generous just to encourage people who have not yet made the step up to Higher level work. Later in the course, marking might be stricter in order to push you harder. Sometimes teachers, knowing the temperament of individual students, may vary marks so that a hard working but struggling student will not be discouraged. And sometimes marks are based accurately on the SQA rules.

How can marking my own work help me improve?

Often teachers don't put a number mark on your essays at all. They write comments providing advice on how to improve. A very good learning exercise is to ask your teacher to provide comments only, and then use the marking scheme in this section to work out what you think your essay is worth. Then ask your teacher if he or she agrees with you. Are you awarding yourself marks that are too low or too high? Understanding WHY you get a certain mark is learning! Being given a mark without understanding why does not help you learn how to improve!

Does my mark depend on the opinion of only one marker?

No. The mark you are awarded by the first SQA marker to read your essays might be reviewed several times. A very experienced panel of markers will check the standard of marking by every single marker. When that happens, individual essays will be read again. If a marker is consistently too generous or severe then all the marks given by the marker will be adjusted.

Sometimes, for a variety of possible reasons, a marker becomes very inconsistent. In that case all the essays marked by that marker will be read and re-marked. Later, if you appeal for a higher award your essays will be marked again, also by an expert panel of markers.

Does the SQA provide advice about what A, B C and D award essays should contain?

Yes, the SQA provides some general advice to markers about marking essays in paper 1.

How do I get an A award?

An A pass essay should have a clear structure with a beginning, middle and end.

It must have accurate, detailed and relevant information. You must USE the information to argue a case or comment on information rather than just regurgitate it as a story. Your answer should show awareness of different points of view which you should evaluate within your answer as part of the process of coming to a balanced conclusion. It is useful but not absolutely necessary to refer to different viewpoints of historians. This is called historiography and points of view are often contradictory. Reaching different viewpoints and arguing about them is what historians do! Finally, you must have a conclusion which sums up your argument / ideas and answers the main question.

What does a B award look like?

A B pass essay is also likely to have a clear structure with a beginning, middle and end.

There must be detailed and relevant information but a few inaccuracies might be forgiven. There should be frequent linkage to the main question and there might be some historiography or use of external evidence. B pass essays tend to be strong on storytelling rather than developed argument. Write an essay packed with detail that mainly tells a relevant story linked to the question and you will get a B.

Why will an essay get a C award?

A C award essay will have a basic simple structure with a short introduction just listing some main points. The middle section will tend to be a collection of information rather than structured and planned. The C award essay will rely heavily on storytelling with very little analysis. Within the C award essay there is likely to be some irrelevance and some inaccuracies. However, the essay will attempt to answer the question set, it will show a basic knowledge of subject content and there will be a weak conclusion making an overall link back to the main question.

What sort of essay will get a D award?

A D award (it just fails to pass) essay will usually have a weak introduction which hardly, if at all, refers to the question or suggests any ideas that will be developed in the essay. There will be a middle section which is mainly a jumbled collection of information with almost no analysis – just storytelling. There will be frequent irrelevancies and inaccuracies. The essay might not even answer the original question and there will probably not be a conclusion. Overall the writer of a D award essay will have very little knowledge about the topic.

Can I get a summary of all the things I need in an essay to make sure of a good pass?

Yes, here it is! You can copy the grid on page 46 and use it as a guide for your essay writing. You can also give this to your teacher to allow him or her to give you feedback on your essay. You will then be able to see what particular parts of your essay need to be improved. Don't be afraid to use your box for comment either to show your teacher where you might have concerns or to comment back to your teacher once the essay has been marked. By discussing what each of you think about the essay, it is usually possible to understand why it gained the mark it got and how that can be improved upon. That's called 'formative assessment' and teachers are becoming very keen on it!

Essay feedback - Higher History name ....

Topic [   ]

Introduction

Good pass ☐
You make clear you understand the topic and task required.
There is a fluent style in which you signpost the main ideas you will develop later.
Your ideas are comprehensive and relevant.
You might indicate different points of view relevant to the main issue.

Pass ☐☐☐
You tend to list the main points you will develop in a straightforward way.
Your points are relevant.

Borderline / fail ☐☐☐☐
An important idea or main point might be left out.
There is not much indication of differing points of view, or analyses.

☐☐☐☐
A very limited reference to topic and task.
Little evidence of planning or logical thought.
Main ideas are left out.
Your introduction is inappropriate in content and/or style.

Paragraph structure

Good pass ☐☐☐
You have an introductory sentence for each paragraph.
You develop one main point per paragraph.
Your paragraph ends with a clear, relevant link back to the main question.

Pass ☐☐☐☐
You usually start with an introductory sentence.
The relevance of each paragraph to the question is usually clear.
Each paragraph is developed with appropriate information.
Your paragraph usually ends with a link back to the main question.

Borderline / fail ☐☐☐
There are few separate or developed paragraphs.
They are poorly developed with unlinked or irrelevant narrative.
Your paragraphs have none / very few links to the main question.

Your comment

Development

Good pass ☐☐   ☐☐   ☐☐☐☐☐   ☐☐☐☐☐
Your information is detailed, accurate and relevant.
Your subject specific vocabulary is very accurate and correctly used.
You make regular clear links between the content of each paragraph and the main question.
You make good use of primary and secondary source evidence.

Pass
You tend to tell a story rather than analysing the main question.
Your information is mostly accurate and relevant.
You make the links between your information and the main question.
Your subject specific vocabulary is usually accurate and appropriately used.
You make some use of primary and secondary source evidence.

Borderline / fail
Your information lacks accuracy / relevance / planning.
Your information is presented as a very simple story.
There are very few attempts to link your information to the main question.
Your subject specific vocabulary lacks accuracy / relevance / is lacking.
You make no use of primary and secondary source evidence.

Conclusion

Good pass ☐☐   ☐   ☐☐   ☐☐☐
Your conclusion answers the main question.
It sums up the main ideas in your argument.
You prioritise your main points in support of your answer with reasons for your decision.

Pass
Your conclusion attempts to sum up the main points in a straightforward way.
It makes a simple comment which makes clear your answers to the main question.

Borderline / fail
You do not sum up the main points in your answer.
It does not contain an overall answer to the main question.
There is no adequate conclusion.

Teacher comment

3

Higher History Paper 2

INTRODUCTION

The Higher History paper 2 exam paper contains the sources and questions for all the special topics studied for Higher – but do not worry. You only have to deal with one special topic.

What are the special topics?

There are nine special topics in total spread over the Medieval, Early Modern and Later Modern options. They are:

1 Norman Conquest and expansion 1050–1153
2 The Crusades 1096–1204
3 Scotland 1689–1715
4 The Atlantic Slave Trade
5 The American Revolution
6 Patterns of Migration: Scotland 1830s–1930s
7 Appeasement and the Road to War, to 1939
8 The Origins and Development of the Cold War 1945–1985
9 Ireland 1900–1985: a Divided Identity

Do I have to choose which special topic to answer?

No. Your teacher / tutor will have made the decision which special topic you study. You have only studied one of them. Most schools and colleges teach options 7, 8, 9, 6 or 2.

What do I have to do?

In paper 2 you will be asked five questions based on five sources and your exam paper will have this instruction on the first page: 'Answer questions from only one special topic. You are expected to use background knowledge appropriately in answering source based questions.'

Should I read this chapter all at once?

No! This chapter shows you how to deal with the different types of questions you will find in paper 2. Wait until you are working on that particular type of question, and then use the advice to help you learn or revise from.

What if the examples given here are not from the special study I am learning about?

Don't worry. Of course the facts, names and events in your special study might be different but the same techniques for answering the type of question applies to all special topics. However, the examples given here apply to over 90 per cent of the candidates sitting Higher History.

THE IMPORTANCE OF SOURCES

What is a source based question?

Each special study will provide you with five sources, some primary and some secondary. Some may be visual, for example a drawing, photograph or a cartoon, but most will be text based.

After the five sources there are five questions based on the sources. That is true no matter what special topic you study. It is the same for everybody.

Three of the questions will target an individual source each but one question will ask about two of the sources and one of the questions will ask you to deal with three of the sources.

Each source based question will require you to use a specific skill in answering them, such as comparing or evaluating.

What are sources?

Sources mean sources of information. They are extracts from historical documents or from history books written after the events they describe. During your course of study you will have seen lots of sources, some primary, some secondary. Some of them are written; sometimes they are maps, photos, cartoons and even poems and songs. All of these sources tell you something about how people felt at the time or what historians thought afterwards.

Why are sources called primary or secondary?

A primary source is any source produced around the time of the event described or shown in the source. Primary sources can also include opinions or descriptions written by people who were alive at the time but who produced the source later – such as autobiographies or memoirs based on diaries kept at the time.

People not directly involved in the events they describe – and usually many years later – produce secondary sources. Clearly, historians writing about the Crusades were not alive hundreds of years ago. They have researched their subject, probably using primary sources to produce their work on the subject.

Are primary sources better than secondary sources?

No, not always. A primary source might let you know how someone felt at the time but what if their understanding of an event or their knowledge was limited? Primary sources might also be biased and written from a particular point of view.

A secondary source usually has the advantage of hindsight and research and the producer of the source is more likely to be objective and unbiased.

In short, all the sources you are given are useful in the context of the exam and it is often your task to evaluate both the content and the opinions in the source. But more of that later.

Why are we given sources in the exam?

History is not just about what we can remember from books. History is about the past, so we need evidence to help us find out about the past. Sources are the raw materials of history. Historians have skills and to be successful in Higher History you are expected to be able to use these skills of analysis in reaching balanced answers to questions using the available evidence, both from the sources provided and your own knowledge. The five different questions in paper 2 test your skills as a historian.

THE RACE AGAINST TIME – PAPER 2

How much time do I have to complete paper 2?

In paper 2 timing is vital – but plan for it and use it to your advantage.

The paper 2 examination lasts for 1 hour 25 minutes (85 minutes) and your target is to answer all five questions in that time.

How many marks is paper 2 worth?

Paper 2 is worth a total of 30 marks.

Each of the five questions has its own number of marks indicated after the question. One of the questions will be worth 8 marks, the others will usually be worth between 4 and 6 marks. You will not get questions worth less than 4 marks.

How can I make sure I give enough time to each question?

There are 30 marks worth of questions to answer in 85 minutes so that is almost three minutes a mark.

If you allow two minutes per mark to write your answers that means you will write for 60 minutes and that that will give you 25 minutes throughout the exam just to READ and THINK.

Do simple multiplication – if you have a 5 mark question you should WRITE for ten minutes. That's one page of A4. (Your 8 mark question should last for 16 minutes – about 1.5 pages.)

As a guide, when you start paper 2 find the point in your question paper where 15 marks worth of questions have been asked. It will not be a perfect division but it will be somewhere around question 3. Make a mark on your question paper to show you where you should be when 42 minutes have passed. The half-way point in your exam is 42 minutes. Don't race to beat this timer. Pace yourself. You might want to quarter the mark distribution to break the exam into 21 minute chunks if you feel it will help you. Remember writing for two minutes per mark STILL LEAVES 25 MINUTES SURPLUS FOR READING!

Should I skip a question if I am unsure of the answer?

No. If you write nothing the only thing a marker can do is to give you nothing. Markers will give you marks even if you have not directly answered the question. If you can select relevant extracts from the source and even give a very simple answer to the questions such as 'This source is partly useful because the source says ...', then you will get one or two marks. Give a marker a chance to give you marks! Never leave a question unanswered.

What will the source based questions be like?

Each of the five questions test different skills such as evaluation and comparison. The rest of this chapter gives advice about how to answer the types of question you will be asked in paper 2.

How will the questions be marked?

Paper 2 questions are skills based. This means you must use the sources to help you answer the questions. You must also do the task you are asked to do. For example, in a comparison question you must compare and in the evaluation questions you must evaluate (or judge) then reach a decision. However, there is a fairly basic guide to marking used by markers to get a rough idea of what mark should be awarded before the precise detail of each question is looked at. Here it is.

The first thing to remind you of is that if you write nothing you will get nothing. It may seem obvious but just by writing a few lines you could gain some marks, even if you think you do not know the answer. Here are the three mark descriptions used.

● If a candidate has selected some relevant evidence from the source OR has used some relevant recalled knowledge but has NOT really answered the question a marker can still award 1 or 2 marks.

● If a candidate has selected relevant evidence from the source AND used some relevant recalled knowledge AND has reached a very basic evaluation (such as 'this source is partly useful but not entirely') a marker can award 3 or 4 marks out of a total of 5 or 6. For 4 marks a marker would be looking for a much better evaluation than the example in this paragraph.

● If a candidate makes clear he or she has understood the main points made in the source AND uses relevant recalled knowledge AND reaches an appropriate and balanced conclusion which does what the question has asked then a marker can award a total of 5 or 6 out of 6.

For the 8 mark question the marks are scaled up, so for the first mark description 2 or 3 marks may be awarded. For the second mark description 4–5 marks may be awarded. For the third mark description 6–8 marks may be awarded.

THE EVALUATION QUESTIONS – PART 1

What is an evaluation question?

The five questions in your paper 2 are all evaluation questions. That means you will be asked to use your own knowledge and the source content to reach a decision, such as how useful or how typical or how reliable a source is. You could also be asked how fully a source explains something. You will also be asked to compare sources.

What is a 'how useful' question?

You will usually get one question that asks you to evaluate the usefulness or value of a source for a particular purpose. Here is a selection of past questions:

Example 1

> How valuable is source B as evidence of public opinion at
> the time of the Anschluss? (special topic 7)

Example 2

> How useful is source A in explaining Warsaw Pact concerns over the situation in Berlin in 1961? (special topic 8)

Example 3

> How valuable is source D as evidence of King Richard's reasons for negotiating a truce with Saladin at the end of the Third Crusade? (special topic 2)

You will see that all questions of this type ask you to judge or evaluate the use of a source for a specific purpose.

Example 1 asks about the value of source A for finding out about public opinion. Example 2 asks how useful the source is as information about the feelings of the Warsaw Pact over the Berlin crisis. Example 3 asks the value of a source for finding out about King Richard's motives in negotiating a truce.

That might seem like stating the obvious but two points must be emphasised here. First, most candidates lose marks by misreading a question and not doing what they are asked. Secondly, the other main loss of marks comes from a failure to use your own knowledge to develop your answer.

Must I always evaluate using my own knowledge as well as the source?

Yes! In this sort of question recalled knowledge is vital. In example 2 for instance, it is impossible to judge the usefulness of a source about the Warsaw Pact and the Berlin Crisis unless it is known what the crisis was about, who or what the Warsaw Pact was and how it felt about the crisis. Who produced the source and when should also trigger some thoughts from your own knowledge.

What does 'how valuable' or 'how useful' mean?

How useful is this photograph?

It would be almost impossible even to begin to answer this question because you have no idea what use is to be made of the picture.

So in any question you must be very careful to read and understand the whole question – and questions can vary.

For example, the same picture of Prime Minister Chamberlain could be used with very different 'how useful' questions such as:

> **How useful is the photograph as evidence of 20th century photo journalism?**

> **How valuable is the photograph for finding out how fashion changed in the 20th century?**

> **How useful is the photograph for finding out about the Munich Agreement of September 1938?**

Clearly the answers would be very different but they are all evaluation questions based on the same source.

In this sort of question 'valuable' and 'useful' mean the same thing. You are being asked to judge the source's usefulness to a historian trying to find out information. In this type of question you are not being asked about the content of the source but how much trust you can have in the source to give information about a topic.

What does evaluate mean?

The question in the exam comes with some helpful advice. Usually it states: 'In reaching a conclusion you should refer to the origins and possible purpose of the source; the content of the source; recalled knowledge.' But it might be easier and more helpful to base your answers around certain questions you should ask about a source as you evaluate it. The most straightforward are

WHO produced the source or WHERE does it come from? In what way is that relevant to assessing the value of a source?

WHAT is the source and how is that relevant to the question?

WHEN was the source produced and how might that clue assist the evaluation of the source?

WHY was the source produced? What were the motives of the producer of the source?

What is meant by a balanced answer?

In any evaluation question the sources will seldom be entirely valuable or useful. They will have limitations and it's up to you to explain what these limits to usefulness are. In this case a useful word to use is PARTLY! By answering that a source is partly useful you have the opportunity to develop points provided in or about the source but you can also include relevant information from your own knowledge which further develops points in the source.

EXAM EXAMPLE 1

Now, before you do a full question try out an example of a short evaluation question based on the background for special topic 7: Appeasement and the Road to War, 1939. This is not a real past paper question, but it is a good introduction to evaluation questions.

This question is worth 4 marks. First, here is the source:

The following extract is from a German newspaper sold on the 28 June 1919.

Vengeance!

German nation!

Today in the Hall of Mirrors at Versailles a disgraceful treaty is being signed. Never forget it! Today German honour is dragged to the grave. Never forget it! The German people will push forward to reconquer their place among the nations of the world. There will be vengeance for the shame of 1919.

Now, here is the question.

> **How useful is this source for finding out about German foreign policy in the 1930s?**
> **In reaching a conclusion you should refer to the origins and possible purpose of the source; the content of the source; recalled knowledge.**

Here is a weak answer to the question.

This source is useful because it refers to revenge for the Treaty of Versailles. Hitler wanted to destroy the Treaty of Versailles which is called 'the shame of 1919'. It refers to the disgrace caused by the treaty and says, 'German honour is dragged to the grave'. It shows German policy was aggressive because it says Germans must 'reconquer their place' and 'There will be vengeance'.

Why is this a weak answer?

This answer is weak mainly because it fails to evaluate by referring to the origins and possible purpose of the source. It simply describes the source. It makes claims that German policy was aggressive but uses very little recall to support that view other than stating that Hitler wanted to destroy the treaty. There is no conclusion providing a balanced answer. This answer would only gain 1 mark as it has not done enough to pass a question which asks the candidate to evaluate the usefulness of the source.

Here is a much better answer.

This source is partly useful for finding out about German foreign policy in the 1930s but it is very limited.

The source is from a German newspaper written in response to the publication of the Treaty of Versailles. Germans were shocked and horrified by the Treaty which punished Germany for starting World War One. Germans did indeed want revenge and this writer is trying to develop an aggressive desire for revenge which did run through German foreign policy in the 1930s.

Clearly the source is a pro German point of view and is therefore biased, referring as it does to 'German honour being dragged to the grave' and a 'disgraceful' treaty. However that is what many Germans felt and one of the attractions of the Nazis in their rise to power was their promise to destroy the Treaty and much of Hitler's foreign policy in the 1930s was aimed at doing that. However the source provides little detail of the policy in the 30s and makes no reference to rearmament, remilitarising the Rhineland, Anschluss or expanding Germany's frontiers, all of which the treaty banned but which happened in the 1930s.

Overall the source gives the background to German foreign policy and a starting point for understanding the policy that followed but no detail of that policy.

Why is this a much better answer?

This answer is much better because it evaluates the source by referring to its origins and possible purpose. It also links the answer back to the original question several times. It uses a lot of recall to show knowledge of policy in the 1930s and how that was linked to the treaty. It reaches a balanced conclusion that correctly explains why the source is only of limited use for finding out about German foreign policy 15 years later. This answer could gain full marks.

EXAM EXAMPLE 2

Now try the same practice again, only this time using a source from paper 2 special topic 8 – The Origins and Development of the Cold War 1945–1985.

Here is the question. It is example 2 from the beginning of this chapter.

> **How useful is source A in explaining Warsaw Pact concerns over the situation in Berlin in 1961? (special topic 8)**
> **The answer to this question is worth 5 marks. In reaching a conclusion you should refer to: the origins and possible purpose of the source; the content of the source; recalled knowledge.**

Source A: from a Declaration of the Warsaw Pact Powers, 13 August 1961

The Western Powers continue to use West Berlin as a centre of subversive activities against the German Democratic Republic (GDR) and all other socialist countries. They smuggle their agents into the GDR for all sorts of subversion, recruit spies and incite hostile elements to organise sabotage and provoke disturbances in the GDR.

Due to the aggression of the reactionary forces of the German Federal Republic and its NATO allies, the Warsaw Pact member states must take necessary measures to guarantee their security and, especially, the security of the GDR in the interests of the German people themselves.

The governments of the Warsaw Pact member states propose to establish an order on the borders of West Berlin which will securely block the way to the subversive activity against the socialist countries. In this way reliable safeguards and effective control can be established around the whole territory of West Berlin, including its border with East Berlin.

Here is a weak answer to the question.

The source is useful because it is from the Warsaw Pact powers. It is a primary source from 1961.

The Warsaw Pact blame the west for causing trouble such as 'subversive activities' and smuggling spies into the GDR.

The source says that Warsaw Pact must take action to protect the GDR against 'aggression of reactionary forces'.

The source is explaining why the Berlin Wall was built to 'securely block the way to the subversive activity against the socialist countries.'

Why is this a weak answer?

There is very little evaluation. It states the source is useful but fails to explain why it is useful. Instead, the answer tends to describe the source and selects some evidence from the source that is relevant but is not then used to evaluate the source. It fails to identify that the source is biased or make any comment about the way the source was written. Although the answer does recognise this is about the building of the Berlin Wall there is almost no other piece of recall. This answer would gain possibly 2 marks for selecting information from the source and some very shallow attempts at evaluation but would not pass so it could NOT gain 3 marks.

Here is a much better answer to the same question.

This source, produced by the communist Warsaw Pact, is useful to an extent but is a one sided, biased viewpoint.

It is written during the Cold War crisis in Berlin leading to the building of the Berlin Wall in 1961.

Berlin had been divided between the victorious allies at the end of World War Two and West Berlin was in the heart of East Germany but the Warsaw Pact believed West Berlin was a centre for spies – 'The Western Powers continue to smuggle their agents into the GDR for all sorts of subversion.'

The Warsaw Pact wanted to justify their actions and claimed they were forced to build the wall by 'the aggression of the reactionary forces of the German Federal Republic and its NATO allies'.

On the other hand the source does not make clear other concerns of the Warsaw Pact. First, East Berlin was used as an 'escape' point for many people wanting to start a new life in the west. Over three million people had escaped into West Berlin. Secondly, the Warsaw Pact was also concerned about the prosperity gap between west and east. Workers from the east could see the higher standard of living in the west and wanted to be part of it. Thirdly, the Warsaw Pact does not mention that while the west was a successful democracy the communist states used force to control its people and was very unpopular.

Finally, the Warsaw pact was concerned they were losing the propaganda war and although they claimed the wall was defensive, most world opinion saw the wall as a way of imprisoning the people inside East Berlin.

In conclusion, the source is of limited value, only showing a biased, selective set of reasons presented by the Warsaw Pact for building the wall.

Why is this a much better answer to the question?

This answer combines recall with effective use of quotes to reach a full evaluation of the source. The answer deals with the origins of the source by explaining where the source came from and the historical background that led to the Warsaw Pact producing the source. The answer also identifies bias in the source and indicates this is an attempt by the Warsaw Pact countries to justify their actions. This deals with the instruction to comment on the purpose of the source. The content of the source is explained and used to back up points made in the answer. There is also a large amount of recalled knowledge here which is used to do two things. First, recalled knowledge sets the scene by explaining the background to the building of the wall. Secondly, recall is used to provide a balanced answer by explaining other reasons for building the wall which the Warsaw Pact statement chose to ignore since they would have reflected badly on the Warsaw Pact.

This answer could reasonably expect to gain full marks.

Helpful hint

This is quite a long answer but as you will see in the section on timing your answers, since the question is worth 5 marks you should realistically expect to write an answer lasting ten minutes. And most people can easily write one side of A4 in ten minutes.

EXAM EXAMPLE 3

Finally, this last example is a full scale example of a question on special topic 7: Appeasement and the Road to War, to 1939.

> **How valuable is source B as evidence of public opinion at the time of the Anschluss?**
> **The answer to this question is worth 5 marks. In reaching a conclusion you should refer to: the origins and possible purpose of the source; the content of the source; recalled knowledge.**

Source B: from an article in the Daily Worker, the newspaper of the British Communist Party, 12 March 1938

British people must act. The struggle for British peace and democracy has entered a stage of great tension. In Spain, Franco has launched his offensive. In Austria the great majority of people are heroically fighting for their independence. When are the British people going to pull their weight in this historic struggle?

The British people should be under no illusions. If fascism wins in these countries it will threaten the very existence of democracy in Britain. It is not merely the peace of central Europe that is trembling in the balance. It is the peace of the world.

Here is a very weak answer to the question.

Britain wanted to fight against fascism. People from Britain were fighting in Spain as part of international brigades to stop Nazis. It says, 'In Spain, Franco has launched his offensive'.

Nazis were winning in Austria. It says people there were 'fighting for their independence'. If Britain does not stop Nazis there will be a World War.

Why is this a very weak answer?

It should be clear to you by now that the vital thing to do in any answer is to answer the question. This answer does not answer the question.

The recall used is mostly irrelevant. Some of the answer is factually wrong – most people in Britain did not want to fight. There is no evaluation of the origins and possible purpose of the source or of the content of the source. This answer would be lucky to get any marks at all.

Here is a better, but still weak, answer to the question.

The source is quite useful as evidence of public opinion at the time of the Anschluss.

It is from a British newspaper and says British people must act. The writer is worried that Fascism will spread in Austria and in Spain where a civil war was going on for almost two years and it looked like fascists would win.

The paper wants Britain to fight to save democracy. It says that the peace of the world is threatened and that British people 'must pull their weight'. In conclusion the source is useful as evidence of public opinion because it shows what some people thought.

Why is this still a weak answer?

At first glance this answer seems reasonable since it refers to the question, quotes from the source, uses some recall and states an opinion about the usefulness of the source. However, this answer does not really evaluate the value of the source. Instead it tends to describe the content of the source and explain what the writer of the source thought.

There is little use made of the origin or possible purpose of the source apart from saying that the source wants British people to fight to save democracy. At most this answer would gain 3 marks.

Here is a much better answer.

The source is partly valuable as evidence of public opinion at the time of the Anschluss.

It is from a British newspaper so shows some British opinion.

It is from March 12, 1938 which is the time of the Anschluss and was written to persuade Britain to get involved in trying to save Austria from Nazi control – 'British people must act…' and 'When are the British people going to pull their weight in this historic struggle?' The report believes taking action to save Austria was part of 'The struggle for British peace and democracy'. When this source was written it seemed as if democracy was fighting for its life in Spain and it looked as if Franco's fascists would win.

On the other hand, the source only shows a minority opinion. It is from the Daily Worker the newspaper of the British Communist Party – a small political group in Britain that was not representative of either the British public or the government.

In fact most of the public did not see what the fuss was about. They wanted no involvement in Anschluss, believing that Austria was more or less German anyway. They thought Anschluss only broke the treaty of Versailles which they felt was unfair and had been broken many times earlier – so was not a reason to fight.

In conclusion, the source is only partly valuable in showing some British opinion but makes no attempt to indicate the majority opinion in Britain at the time.

Why is this a much better answer?

This is a good answer, which does exactly what is required, and makes use of the source and the advice within the question to reach an appropriate conclusion. The origin, purpose and content are all fully developed and recalled knowledge is used throughout the answer. Quotes from the source are included to support the evaluation and not used simply to describe the source. This answer could gain full marks.

What are the essential tips for answering this type of question?

- You never get sources which are entirely useless!
- Don't just describe the source – that's not evaluating!
- Make sure your answer refers to all the advice points provided with the question.
- Provide a balanced answer which analyses the source and includes your own knowledge.
- Make sure your evaluation does what you are asked to do in the question.

THE COMPARISON QUESTION

Am I likely to be asked a comparison question?

Yes. You will always get a comparison or compare question in your paper 2 exam. Sometimes the question will obviously be a comparison question because it will use the word 'compare' in the question, such as 'Compare the views expressed in sources A and B on ...' or 'Compare the explanations in sources B and C about ...'.

You will also see that the comparison can be between any two sources within your special topic section in the exam paper. It doesn't have to be A and B. It could refer to sources C or D or even E.

How do I spot a comparison question?

Comparison questions can also be a bit disguised when the word compare does NOT appear in the question. However, they are easy to spot because they are the only question out of the five you will be doing that will refer to TWO sources in the question – such as 'To what extent do sources C and D agree about ...?'

What does compare mean?

A comparison question requires you to make clear connections and comparisons between sources. The skill being assessed is your ability to compare and that does not mean your ability to describe two sources. Look at this example to see what I mean.

Your question here is compare girl A with girl B.

A weak answer would be to describe each girl in turn.

Girl A has long blonde hair. She is skinny. She has a light coloured top on and a short skirt. She has matching shoes and is tall.

Girl B has dark curly hair. She is plump. She has a dark top on and baggy trousers. She is not very tall.

Why is this a weak answer?

Because the candidate does not demonstrate the skill of comparing. What is written here is a correct description of the two girls but at no point is there any comparison.

A much better answer would be like this.

Overall, A and B are quite different although there is one similarity. They both seem to be girls.

In detail, girl A has long blonde hair but girl B has dark curly hair. Girl A is much skinnier than girl B is. The clothes they wear are also different. A is wearing a light coloured top with a short skirt and matching shoes whereas B has on a dark top and baggy trousers. A has light coloured shoes, B has dark shoes.

Why is this a much better answer?

In this answer there are FOUR points of detailed comparison – hair, body shape, clothes and shoes. You will also notice there is an overall comparison in that the answer identifies one similarity – they are both girls.

This is exactly what the exam requires you to do. In your exam the comparison question will have as part of its 'helpful hint' the following phrase – 'Compare the content overall and in detail.'

Should I organise my answer round the words 'overall' and 'in detail'?

Yes. Make it easy for a marker to give you marks by following the recommended style of answering. Start your answer with the word 'Overall' and then identify the main difference between the sources. For example, in the Appeasement and the Road to War section you will probably get a source FOR appeasement and one AGAINST it. So your answer could start: 'Overall, Source A supports a policy of appeasement while source B is opposed to it.' Then you should use the phrase 'In detail' and then write the rest of your answer comparing the sources point by point.

Take one point from the source and show how it is supported or disagreed with by the other source. Keep going to and fro between the sources until you have finished comparing them. If you want a good mark it is not enough just to quote a sentence from one source then compare by quoting from another. By all means do that as part of your answer, but you should also explain the point being made by your extracts in your own words. That is what is meant by a developed comparison.

Should I use recall like the other answers in the paper?

No, the comparison question is the only question in paper 2 where you do NOT HAVE TO use recalled information in your answer. All the marks can be gained from comparing the sources so if a comparison question has 5 marks then it is wise to make at least five direct comparisons. However, it is often useful to use recall to set the scene – historians call it placing the sources in context – but do it briefly! You will not lose marks by including recall and credit can be given for appropriate extra information!

EXAM EXAMPLE 4

Here is your first practice comparison question from special topic 7: Appeasement and the Road to War, to 1939. It's a shortened version of a real question used a few years ago. This version is worth 3 marks.

> **Compare the attitudes towards the German occupation of Austria in March 1938 contained in sources B and C.**
>
> **Compare the content overall and in detail.**

Source B: from a letter to his sister by Lord Tweedsmuir, Governor General of Canada, 14 March 1938

 I do not myself quite see what there is to fuss about. Austria will be much more comfortable, economically under Germany's wing.

Source C: from a speech by Winston Churchill, MP, in the House of Commons, March 1938

 We cannot leave the Austrian question where it is – a small country brutally struck down, its government scattered to the winds.

Here is a weak answer to the question.

 Source B says that there is no fuss and Austria is OK being looked after by Germany. Source C says there is a problem and Austria has been attacked and destroyed by Germany.

Why is this a weak answer?

There is no comparison – there is no connection between the two sources and the answer simply describes each source in turn. Nor is there any attempt to answer the question overall and in detail.

Here is a much better answer.

This brief introduction shows how to set the scene.

 In March 1938 Nazi armies occupied Austria which was absorbed into the German Reich. This was Anschluss, forbidden by the Treaty of Versailles.

Overall source B supports appeasement by suggesting no action is necessary while source C believed appeasement is wrong, Germany is in the wrong and something should be done about Anschluss. **[1 mark so far!]**

In detail Lord Tweedsmuir's (source B) opinion was that he failed to 'see what there is to fuss about' whereas Churchill believed, 'We cannot leave the Austrian question where it is'. Tweedsmuir thought it was not a serious issue but Churchill did. **[your second mark]**

Lord Tweedsmuir believed that Austria 'will be much more comfortable, ... under Germany's wing' whereas Churchill said Austria was – a small country brutally struck down, its government scattered to the winds'. Tweedsmuir suggests Austria accepts Anschluss as a helpful thing while Churchill believes Austria has been taken over by force and against the wishes of Austrians. **[your third mark]**

Why is this a much better answer?

You will see that this example of an answer does not just copy down the sources. It does TWO main things. One is that relevant parts of the source have been selected and used. The SECOND thing is that each time a comparison is made there is also a short comment from the candidate to make clear the point being made.

EXAM EXAMPLE 5

Now try the same practice again, only this time using sources from paper 2 special topic 8 – The Origins and Development of the Cold War 1945–1985. This question is worth 3 marks.

> **Compare the attitudes to the Cuban missile crisis expressed in sources A and B.**
>
> **Compare the content overall and in detail.**

Source A: from a television address by President John F Kennedy, 22 October 1962

A series of offensive missile sites is now in preparation on that imprisoned island. The secret and swift build up of communist missiles constitutes an explicit threat to the peace and security of all the Americas.

Source B: from Andrei Gromyko (an important politician in the USSR)

US foreign policy has launched a loud propaganda campaign about 'the Soviet threat' to the Americas. The soviet and Cuban governments reached agreement on the further reinforcement of Cuba's defences. The appropriate arms were installed, including rockets. This was purely a defensive measure.

Here is a weak answer to the question.

Source B says that the Russians are threatening America. It states 'The secret and swift build up of communist missiles constitutes an explicit threat to the peace and security of all the Americas.'

Source B says that Cuba is defending itself. It states, 'This was purely a defensive measure.'

Why is this a weak answer?

There is no comparison – there is no connection between the two sources and the answer simply describes each source in turn and then copies out a large chunk of the source but does not use it for any purpose. Nor is there any attempt to answer the question overall and in detail.

Here is a much better answer.

In 1962 USSR missiles sites were built on Cuba. For the first time US cities would be within range of Russian controlled missiles.

Overall source A by President Kennedy sees Russian actions as aimed against America while Gromyko in source B claims Russia and Cuba's actions are defensive. **[1 mark so far]**

In detail Kennedy refers to 'offensive missile sites now in preparation' while Gromyko speaks of the 'reinforcement of Cuba's defences. **[your second mark]**

Kennedy continues by saying, 'The build up of communist missiles constitutes an explicit threat to the peace and security of all the Americas' while Gromyko describes the missile sites as, 'appropriate arms' intended only as 'a defensive measure. **[your third mark]**

Why is this a much better answer?

As in the previous example, the selection of extracts from the sources are USED to support the comparison and extracts from the sources have been INTERLINKED so that the direct comparisons are obvious to a marker.

EXAM EXAMPLE 6

Now its time to try some full size comparisons.

This example is from special topic option 6, Patterns of Migration: Scotland 1830s–1930s. Here is the question, worth 5 marks:

> **Compare the views of sources B and C concerning the provision of education for Irish immigrants to Scotland.**
>
> **Compare the content overall and in detail.**

Source B: from the report of the Education Commission (Scotland) (1866)

The people in the Clyde district are of the poorest classes and this district has a large mixture of Irish immigrants. For this large Irish element and their needs there exists no school within the district, beyond a private adventure school in one of the wynds. Roman Catholic children are indeed to be found in the other schools but in comparatively small numbers and their attendance is extremely irregular. It is a fact that many children in the Clyde district, both Catholic and Protestant, but chiefly the former, attend no school. What are these neglected children doing then, if they are selling matches and running errands, cared for by no-one, not at school? They are idling in the streets and wynds, tumbling about in the gutters.

Source C: from W Hamish Fraser and RJ Morris (eds), *People and Society in Scotland* Vol.II, 1830–1914 (1990)

The uneven pace of an industrialising and urbanising society was reflected in distinctive religious, cultural and educational divisions. The largest number of schools, pupils and teachers was to be found in Glasgow, but many of those were Catholic schools outside the state system. Irish settlement, especially after the Famine, produced an ever-growing demand for Catholic schools and teachers. Nonetheless, by the 1860s, the Catholic clergy could boast that they had overcome the immense difficulties and could offer pupils instruction in the three Rs and the Bible. But the community lacked the resources to pay adequate school fees or to raise the necessary funds towards teachers' salaries and school buildings. As a result, by the end of the century, there was a growing crisis in Catholic education.

Here is a good answer to the question.

Your answer does not need to be exactly like this but there are 5 marks so you MUST try to get five direct comparisons as this answer has tried to do. Remember there is no recall necessary in a comparison question, and this answer shows how 5 marks can be achieved by using no recall at all.

Overall source B suggests that the provision of education for Irish immigrants was almost non existent and children of Irish immigrants did not want to attend schools. On the other hand source C suggests that the problem was one of supply to meet the demand of an immigrant population that did want a Catholic education. **[first mark]**

In detail source B states there was a lack of educational provision for Irish immigrants in the Clyde area. ('For this large Irish element and their needs there exists no school within the district') whereas source C provides a more positive view about educational provision for Catholic Irish immigrants. ('the Catholic clergy could boast that they had overcome the immense difficulties and could offer pupils instruction in the three Rs and the Bible') **[second mark]**

Source B continues that 'Roman Catholic children are indeed to be found in the other schools but in comparatively small numbers and their attendance is extremely irregular' but source C claims that demand was high for education by writing 'Irish settlement, especially after the Famine, produced an ever-growing demand for Catholic schools and teachers.' **[third mark]**

Source B reports that 'many children in the Clyde district, both Catholic and Protestant, but chiefly the former, attend no school ... They are idling in the streets and wynds, tumbling about in the gutters' while source C argues that by the 1860s Catholic clergy had overcome the huge difficulties and could offer elementary education to all. Demand for schools was so great that 'the community lacked the resources to pay adequate school fees or to raise the necessary funds towards teachers' salaries and school buildings.' The problem was not lack of attendance but lack of places to attend! **[fourth mark]**

Finally source B implies that Catholic children avoided school through choice and did not want education whereas source C suggests that the problem lay with the lack of resources and money to provide schools for growing demand. **[fifth mark]**

EXAM EXAMPLE 7

Finally here is a full scale example of a question on special topic 7: Appeasement and the Road to War, to 1939. This question is worth 5 marks.

> **Compare the views about the Munich settlement expressed in sources A and B.**
>
> **Compare the content overall and in detail.**

Source A: from a letter to the editor, signed 'An Ashamed Peace lover', *The Scotsman*, 1 October 1938

I am sure that on hearing the results of the Munich conference over the wireless in the early hours of Friday morning, thousands of people will be shocked and humiliated. Hitler and Mussolini have got everything they asked for without firing a shot.

Czechoslovakia, the victim, had no opportunity of a say in the deliberations which sealed her fate and our Prime Minister, while willing to spend hours with Hitler, has not thought it worthwhile to have any direct talks with Benes. At the crucial moment Britain and France have shown that they are not willing to fight for Czechoslovakia but they are willing to hand over her industry, property etc. to Hitler as it stands.

Britain and France appear to have thrown Czechoslovakia to the wolves.

Source B: adapted from JF Kennedy, *Why England Slept* (1940)

People felt that Chamberlain was badly taken in, but I think Chamberlain could not have fought even if he had wanted to. I believe that Chamberlain was sincere in thinking that a great step had been taken towards healing one of Europe's problem areas. Most people in Britain felt, 'It's not worth a war to prevent the Sudeten Germans from going back to Germany'. They failed at that time to see the larger issue, involving the domination of Europe. But although all these factors played a part in the settlement of Munich, I feel that Munich was inevitable on the grounds of lack of armaments alone.

Here is a very weak answer to the question.

Both sources are about the Munich settlement. They are about Czechoslovakia.

Source A says 'thousands of people will be shocked and humiliated.' It says, 'Hitler and Mussolini have got everything they asked for without firing a shot.' It says Czechoslovakia was ignored.

Source B says that Britain did not want a war. It says that Chamberlain was 'taken in' and he was a fool.

Why is this a weak answer?

There is no short scene setting introduction. The answer is too short and source B is hardly used. The answer does not compare the sources. There is no attempt to give an overall and a detailed answer. It also contains errors, for example when it states that source B thinks Chamberlain was a fool and 'taken in' by Hitler. In that source the writer is reporting what some people felt. At no point does the author of the source suggest Chamberlain was a fool. For all these reasons this answer would gain at most 2 marks, but probably only 1.

Here is a much better answer.

The sources refer to the Czech crisis of September 1938 when Hitler demanded possession of the Sudetenland and it seemed as if war was likely until an agreement was reached at the Munich conference.

Overall, the main difference is between the 'Ashamed Peace lover' who represents the views of those who were opposed to the Munich agreement and felt Czechoslovakia had been betrayed. On the other hand source B is from a more neutral view one year later and considers the fuller reasons for the Munich agreement

In detail, source A believes 'thousands of people will be shocked and humiliated' but Kennedy (source B) seems more prepared to understand Chamberlain's actions rather than condemn them – 'I think Chamberlain could not have fought even if he had wanted to'.

Source A attacks the Munich agreement by saying 'Hitler and Mussolini have got everything they asked for without firing a shot' but source B takes a realistic view by commenting that 'Munich was inevitable on the grounds of lack of armaments alone' suggesting that Britain was in no position to fire any shots anyway.

Source B considers public opinion and states 'Most people in Britain felt it's not worth a war to prevent the Sudeten Germans from going back to

Germany' and source A regretfully agrees that 'At the crucial moment Britain and France have shown that they are not willing to fight for Czechoslovakia'.

While Kennedy believes 'Chamberlain was sincere', the 'Ashamed Peace lover' condemns Chamberlain by saying 'our Prime Minister, while willing to spend hours with Hitler, has not thought it worthwhile to have any direct talks with Benes.'

In conclusion source A is opposed to the Munich agreement and believes Britain has betrayed Czechoslovakia – 'Britain and France appear to have thrown Czechoslovakia to the wolves' while source B takes a wider, more realistic view and on balance believes 'that Munich was inevitable'.

Why is this a good answer?

The reasons why this is a full answer should be clear – if not, look back at the essential guidance points. Comparison questions don't need recall. However, it is often useful to set the scene – but do it briefly! The scene is set (and some recall used) at the start of the answer in one sentence.

Don't just describe each source. Apart from the first context setting sentence, each following sentence in the answer is balanced with a comparison reference to each source.

Make as many comparisons as there are marks – there are six comparisons in this answer.

Use the words 'overall' and 'in detail' correctly in your answer – they are there making it clear to a marker you are doing what is requested.

What are the essential tips for answering this type of question?

- Compare questions don't need recall.
- Don't just describe each source.
- Make as many comparisons as there are marks.
- Use the words 'overall' and 'in detail' correctly in your answer.

As this answer has what examiners call a developed comparison – in other words the points of comparison are explained in the candidate's own words – then this answer could gain full marks.

THE EVALUATION QUESTIONS – PART 2

This chapter deals with the evaluation question which asks how fully a source explains something. The secret of success is to write a balanced answer. That means you must identify the parts of the source which do help explain and also use your own knowledge to add in other relevant points or explanations which are not in the source. The sources have been carefully chosen and will contain information that does partly explain why certain things happened. The sources are not useless!

However, the sources will never tell the full story so you are expected to use recall to develop your answer further. In all evaluation questions you MUST use recalled information.

How can I recognise this sort of evaluation question?

Usually the question will contain phrases such as 'How fully does the source ...?' or 'To what extent does the source ...?' Here is a selection of past questions, all of which will be analysed in this chapter.

> **How fully does source A reflect public opinion about the remilitarisation of the Rhineland in March 1936? (special topic 7)**

> **To what extent does source E reflect the experiences of Scottish emigrants during the 19th century? (special topic 6)**

> **How fully does Maalouf (source C) illustrate the weakness of the Muslims during the First Crusade? (special topic 2)**

> **How far does source D explain the aims of the reform movement in Czechoslovakia in 1968? (special topic 8)**

What do I need to do to be successful?

First of all you must identify relevant points in the source. Some people get confused with the word 'identify'. It simply means you have to spot relevant information in the source. To make sure a marker knows you have done that, quote your extract briefly in your answer.

Secondly, you should explain what your selection of words from the source means. What points are being made? What ideas or points of view are the writer expressing?

Thirdly, use the word PARTLY! By saying you agree partly, or a source explains something partly, or a source is partly useful you have the opportunity to develop not only points about the source but also points not made by the source but which are still relevant to the question. By using 'partly' you are opening up the question to lead towards a balanced conclusion and also the opportunity to show off recall.

Can I see an example of how to do this type of question?

Yes. First of all look at what might seem at first to be a silly question. It is: 'How fully do you accept the opinion that this desk is grey?'

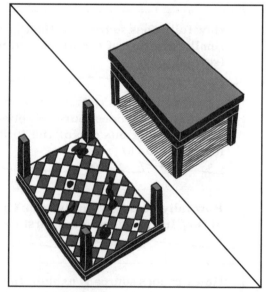

Clearly, 'the desk' shown here is meant to represent any source you might be given.

It's also clear that the desk is not entirely grey so you cannot answer with a simple 'yes'.

Equally clearly, some of the desk IS grey so you cannot answer with a simple 'no'. In other words each source you evaluate will have some correct or useful information in it so you cannot dismiss it as useless. But equally, the source will not have all the information required so you cannot just accept the source as fully useful. The answer lies in the word 'partly'.

Here is a good answer.

The desk is, I agree, partly grey. This is shown by the top surface which is indeed grey. On the other hand the desk is not entirely grey – for example there are black edges and legs which prove the desk is not entirely grey.

On the underside of the desk there is a checker board pattern of black and white and there are things stuck to the desk of varying colours but not identified!

For these reasons I only partly accept the description of the desk as grey.

Why is this a good answer?

This answer deals with the point of the question and recognises much of the desk is grey and details which parts are that colour. The answer is then balanced by identifying parts of the desk which are not grey and defines what shades and colours also exist on the desk.

Finally, the answer reaches a balanced, considered conclusion which links back to the original question.

EXAM EXAMPLE 8

Now try out these ideas with a version of a question from special topic 7: Appeasement and the Road to War, to 1939. This version is worth 6 marks.

> **How fully does source A reflect public opinion about the remilitarisation of the Rhineland in March 1936?**
>
> **Use the source and recalled knowledge.**

Source A: from the *Dundee Courier and Advertiser*, 9 March 1936, referring to Germany's reoccupation of the Rhineland

There can be no doubt in the mind of the country. It will refuse to be led into a new world war. The plain truth is that the Treaty of Versailles is in tatters. It was an imposed Treaty, valid just as long as the country on which it was imposed remained too weak to resist. That time was passed when Germany recreated her army last year. If Germany's revival was to be resisted it should have been resisted then.

Here is a weak answer to the question.

 The source fully shows public opinion in March 1936. It states, 'the country ... will refuse to be led into a new world war' and 'The plain truth is that the Treaty of Versailles is in tatters.' People were against a war and many people did not support the treaty of Versailles. So the source does show public opinion about the remilitarisation of the Rhineland.

Why is this a weak answer?

First of all it is too short. A thorough answer for 6 marks should cover about one page of A4. Secondly, two parts of the source are quoted but without developing the points by using much recall. Other points made in the source about Germany being now too strong to resist are ignored. There is no balance. Many points relevant to the issue and which could have been used to balance the answer are not mentioned in the source. The recall in the answer is very short and needs more accurate explanation. At most this answer would gain 3 marks. The sources are used to an extent and there is a basic evaluation.

Here is a much better answer.

 In March 1936 Hitler remilitarised the Rhineland area of Germany. His action broke the Treaty of Versailles and the Treaty of Locarno, signed in 1925, in which Germany voluntarily agreed to the status of the Rhineland.

Source A reflects partly public opinion about the remilitarisation of the Rhineland.

By writing 'it will refuse to be led into a new world war, the Dundee Courier and Advertiser is referring to the strong anti war feeling in the country.

Britain had been traumatised by the Great War and did not want to repeat it. The Great War had been 'the war to end all wars'.

The public were also worried about a future war in which 'the bomber would always get through'. Gas bombing would put civilians in the front line and thousands would die.

In 1936, 11 million signatures on a peace petition show that source A is quite right.

By writing, 'The plain truth is that the Treaty of Versailles is in tatters', the paper is referring to the many times the treaty has been changed such as the end of reparations, German rearmament, the Anglo German naval treaty and so on. In Britain there was also a strong feeling that the treaty was too harsh and unrealistic and by the 1930s there was a feeling that alteration of the treaty was acceptable.

Finally the paper states 'If her resurgence was to be resisted it should have been resisted then.'

This is a reference to the belief that Germany was now too strong since it rearmed in 1935 and that Britain could do little about it now.

Overall the paper deals with many of the attitudes although it ignores some points.

It does not mention the feeling that social problems in Britain in the 1930s were more pressing and as Lord Lothian said, 'Hitler is only going into his own back garden.' In other words, he was attacking nobody so it was inconceivable that Britain would risk a war when Hitler had used no violence simply to move his own troops within his own country's borders.

Why is this a good answer?

There is a clear introduction which sets the scene, or context, of the source. By doing this the candidate is also showing recalled knowledge, necessary in terms of the question which instructs, 'use the source and recalled knowledge'.

The answer is a much better length and uses effectively quotes from the source to introduce paragraphs which then include recalled knowledge to explain and develop the points made in the answer.

The answer is also balanced by a consideration of points relevant to public opinion at the time but which are not mentioned in the source.

Finally, there is a conclusion which answers the question and ties together the main points in the answer. This is worth full marks.

Is there a detailed process I can follow to write a good evaluation answer?

Yes. There is a simple process you can follow in the evaluation questions that can work if you are worried about this type of question. It can also work as a basis for a very high scoring answer. Here is how to do it.

Before you start writing, pick out what the main points, relevant to the question, are.

First of all, set the context as you saw in the last answer. That should take NO MORE than two sentences. Then move on to dealing with the source. You could write 'The first point made by the source is ...' but be careful. Don't just quote and move on. Always after quoting write 'This means ...' and explain what point is being made by the extract you selected. That's called developing the point. Once you have done that move on to the second point.

Once you have finished developing the points in the source you could write something like 'On the other hand the source does not cover all the points relevant at the time. For example it does not deal with ...' and that gives you a chance to show off your knowledge by explaining relevant points omitted from the source. But please remember the word relevant. Don't try to include everything you know about a topic. Answer the question with the words RELEVANT and TIMING running through your brain. Before you get carried away, look at the number of marks. If it's only 6 marks you should only be writing for about twelve minutes.

Now try to write an answer using this technique. This time there are three examples, from special topic 6 (Patterns of Migration), special topic 2 (The Crusades) and special topic 8 (The Cold War)

EXAM EXAMPLE 9

> **To what extent does source E reflect the experiences of Scottish emigrants during the 19th century? (6 marks)**

Source E: from an interview with Myra Kirkpatrick, a researcher into patterns of migration

Even among the few Scottish convicts, some rapidly became rich in Australia. Among Scottish immigrants the proportion was undoubtedly much higher. There were probably three main reasons for this. Many Scottish migrants were middle class; or tenant farmers. Their Presbyterian faith often came near to equating virtue with material success, but it did instil into their minds the habits of hard work and thrift. And the average standard of education, as much above England's as England was above Ireland's, also gave the Scottish migrants an advantage.

Here is an answer using the process described earlier.

The source partly reflects the experiences of Scots emigrants.

First, the source says even some convicts became rich in Australia. This means after they were freed they could work hard and make money such as running sheep farms. The source says many Scots were used to working hard and being thrifty (saving) their money.

Secondly the source says they became rich for different reasons such as better education, their religion or their experience as farmers in Scotland.

I know that many Scots were successful in different businesses such as banking, farming and shipbuilding abroad. They kept their Scottish identity alive. But I also know many Scots returned home after a short time overseas and were not successful.

So the source shows the positive and good things about Scots emigrants but does not mention the down side where some emigrants did not do well and came home.

Why is this a reasonably good answer?

This does not read like a very good answer but compare it to the marking scheme that allowed 1 or 2 marks if relevant evidence was selected from the source but no evaluation of the source was made. Clearly the source is used, some recall is included and there is an evaluation so it must get at least 3 marks, if not 4 out of 6.

The marking scheme for that number of marks states that relevant evidence is selected from the source and limited recall is used to evaluate the source. This answer does all those things so WILL pass, even if there is not a huge amount of detail.

EXAM EXAMPLE 10

> **How fully does Maalouf (source C) illustrate the weakness of the Muslims during the First Crusade? (6 marks)**

Source C: from A Maalouf, *The Crusades Through Arab Eyes* (1983)

> *The strong man of Cairo vizier al-Afdal had not concealed his satisfaction when in April 1097 ambassadors from Alexius Comnenus had informed him that a massive contingent of Frankish knights had arrived at Constantinople and were about to launch an offensive in Asia Minor.*
>
> *Since the middle of the century Seljuk advances had been eroding the territory of the Fatamid Caliphate and the Byzantine empire alike. Al-Afdal dreamed of a concerted operation by the two allied powers and when he learned that the emperor had received a large reinforcement of troops from the land of the Franks he felt that revenge was at hand.*

> *The delegation he dispatched to the besiegers of Antioch made no mention of a non-aggression pact. That much was obvious thought the vizier. What he proposed to the Franks was a formal partition: northern Syria for the Franks, southern Syria for him.*

Here is a reasonably good answer.

Maalouf's description partly illustrates the weakness of the Muslims during the First Crusade.

First, he says that vizier al-Afdal could not 'conceal his satisfaction' when he heard that crusaders were arriving in Constantinople ready 'to launch an offensive in Asia Minor'. The vizier did not like the Seljuk Turks and was happy they were being attacked.

Secondly it shows how the vizier was prepared to ally with the crusaders against the Seljuks and divide Syria – as a non-aggression pact. 'That much was obvious ... what he proposed ... was a formal partition.'

Clearly the Muslims were divided but the source does not really explain those divisions which were political and religious. Sunni and Shi-ites were divided religiously and politically. The Seljuks had overrun Arab lands in Syria and Baghdad but their empire was starting to break up.

Why is this also a reasonably good answer?

The comment is the same as for example 9 (see page 78).

This answer does enough at least to pass because the source is used, some recall is included and there is an evaluation so it must get at least 3 marks, if not 4 out of 6.

EXAM EXAMPLE 11

> **How far does source D explain the aims of the reform movement in Czechoslovakia in 1968? (6 marks)**

Source D: from the action programme of the Czech Communist Party, April 1968

> *We must reform the whole political system so that it will permit the dynamic development of socialism and democracy.*
>
> *There must be constitutional freedoms of assembly and association this year to meet the needs of all our people. There should be no bureaucratic interference*

or monopoly by any individual organisation. The law must also guarantee freedom of speech for minority interests and opinions. Freedom of movement, particularly travel abroad, for our citizens must be guaranteed by law.

The law must protect the personal rights and property of our citizens. We must remove laws that put individual citizens at a disadvantage with the state and other institutions.

To make the economy more democratic we must ensure the independence of business from state control and the right to choose jobs freely.

Here is a very good answer, but still using the process described earlier.

By 1968 many Czech people supported reform. The new Prime Minister Dubcek seemed to promise a Prague Spring of new hope after the repression of the previous government and control by the USSR.

First, the source says, 'we must reform so that it will permit dynamic development of democracy.' This meant that Dubcek and other reformers wanted to allow democracy to develop within the socialist state and provide what was called 'socialism with a human face'.

Secondly, and connected to allowing democracy, the source states, 'there must be ...' This meant that the people should be freer to meet and discuss outwith the control or 'monopoly' of one organisation, presumably the Communist Party.

Thirdly the source continues, 'the law must guarantee freedoms,' and goes on to detail rights of free speech, even for minority opinion and the right to travel abroad. This means that the reformers are directly challenging the control of the Communist Party which allowed no criticism or minority opinion and tried to prevent people travelling abroad to non-communist countries.

Finally the source demands that 'personal rights and property of citizens' must be protected and that the economy should be free of state interference and control. Again this means the power of the Communist Party would be weakened if the reforms happened.

On the other hand the source does not cover all the points relevant at the time. For example it does not explain why there was such a demand for political reform after the repression of the Novotny regime. It does not mention the discontent among the intellectuals such as writers and artists about the lack of freedom nor does it mention public discontent with the lack of economic progress with low production and high prices.

Finally it does not suggest that at first the USSR was supportive of Dubcek hoping that reforms would increase efficiency, prosperity and so reduce discontent.

In conclusion the source does illustrate the demands without really explaining directly why there were such demands.

Why is this a good answer?

Although this answer uses a predictable process it is a process that works. The relevant points in the source are identified. The source extracts are not just included, they are explained. A lot of recall is used showing off a thorough knowledge of this subject. A conclusion directly answers the question set and sums up how fully the source illustrated the growing demand for reform and draws a thoughtful distinction between illustrating the demand and explaining the reasons.

What are the essential tips for answering this type of question?

- Remember that the source will be partly useful.
- It will not provide all the information you need.
- Identify relevant points from the source relevant to the question asked.
- Use relevant recall to mention points that are not in the source but are relevant to the answer.
- Reach a conclusion which refers exactly to what the question asks.

EVALUATING PICTURE QUESTIONS

This section shows how to deal with a question based on illustrations.

In recent years illustrations such as pictures, drawings, cartoons, posters and maps have all been used in some of the special study options of paper 2. These questions often ask you to set a cartoon or illustration in context and then analyse it, making clear the meaning of the illustration or the intention of the artist.

What does setting in context mean?

An illustration or cartoon or drawing starts life as an idea. The artist, cartoonist or even photographer then uses their ideas to produce the illustration. But what gives them the idea? What events happened which caused the artists to think as they did and caused the illustration to be produced?

The secret of a good answer to 'a picture question' lies in knowing what the illustration is about and what point of view the artist has about the event.

How do I know what event the illustration is about?

Every source in the exam comes with a brief introduction outlining where the source comes from and when it was produced. This information is always useful in letting you know what the source is about. For example in special topic 7 (Appeasement) a cartoon or picture dated March 1936 will almost certainly be about German reoccupation of the Rhineland. Likewise in special topic 8 (Cold War) a cartoon dated 1961 will probably be about a crisis in Berlin. Other pictures may illustrate wider themes within the topic, such as the example you will see about later 19th century Scotland. You will always be given enough information about an illustration to decide what it is about.

Must I use my own knowledge in this answer?

Yes. It is never enough just to describe what you see in the illustration. You MUST use your own knowledge to develop the points in the cartoon or illustration. That means you must explain in detail the points shown or hinted at in the illustration.

Write an answer long enough to make as many developed points as there are marks for the question.

EXAM EXAMPLE 12

Here is a question from special topic 7: Appeasement and the Road to War, to 1939.

> **To what extent does the cartoon illustrate Chamberlain's policy during the Czech crisis of 1938? (6 marks)**
>
> **Use the source and recalled knowledge.**

This cartoon appeared in *The News of the World*, 25 September 1938

Here is a weak answer.

The cartoon from Punch shows Chamberlain pushing a globe over a cracking plank. The plank is called Czech crisis and is about Germany wanting to take over Czechoslovakia. The Prime Minister is stuck on the plank and is about to fall onto rocks called war.

Why is this a weak answer?

There is no scene setting introduction. This answer really just describes the content of the cartoon without explaining its point or the significance / meaning of all the features in the cartoon. There is almost no recall – the only small piece of knowledge is that Chamberlain was British Prime Minister. There is also a factual error. Hitler did not want to take over Czechoslovakia in September 1938 – the crisis was over one area of Czechoslovakia called the Sudetenland. At no point in the answer is there any direct answer to the question.

This answer might gain 2 marks out of 6. The marking instructions offer between 1 and 2 marks for selecting relevant evidence from the source and / or providing some recalled information but without making the required evaluation.

How should a good answer be constructed?

Follow these steps to answer any cartoon / illustration question.

1 Check the date. It is September 1938. That should tell you the topic is the Czech crisis which came to a head at that time.

2 Check the source. It is from Punch, a British magazine, therefore likely to show a British point of view.

3 Check any characters / figures in the cartoon. The figure is Chamberlain, British Prime Minister, and the person who most represented appeasement.

4 Check the words in the cartoon. They are 'Czech crisis', 'peace', 'war', 'chaos'. They are there for a reason – explain the reasons.

5 What other features can you see in the cartoon? Crumbling cliffs, jagged rocks, a globe being pushed over a narrow plank that is breaking up. Chamberlain has his sleeves rolled up. There are dark clouds in the top right of the cartoon. The cartoonist has chosen to include these features for a reason. It is your task to explain what they mean and why the cartoonist included them.

Here is a much better answer.

In September 1938 British Prime Minister Chamberlain flew three times within two weeks to meet Hitler. His intention was to avoid a major war breaking out over a crisis in the Sudetenland, an area of Czechoslovakia.

This cartoon from Punch shows Chamberlain working hard to avoid war, represented by his sleeves being rolled up. In reality Chamberlain was an elderly man who flew to three separate meetings with Hitler in September. Each time Chamberlain thought he had agreement but Hitler kept increasing pressure until finally a settlement of sorts was reached at Munich.

The crisis is represented by the jagged rocks called war onto which the world would fall if Chamberlain fails. The difficulty of the task is shown by a narrow, cracking plank.

Chamberlain is shown to be attempting to save the world from war (the clouds and 'chaos' behind him) but success is nor certain since the cliff edge of 'peace' is crumbling.

On balance the cartoon illustrates Chamberlain's policy during the Czech crisis of 1938 fairly well. It gives the impression of imminent crisis and Chamberlain's role in personally trying to maintain peace. However by itself the cartoon gives little precise information about Chamberlain's methods, motivations or the discussions which took place.

Why is this a good A pass answer?

There is a scene setting introduction which contains important detailed recall. The answer not only describes the content of the cartoon but also explains all the features in the cartoon by linking them to the Czech crisis of 1938. Finally there is a direct answer to the question.

This answer would gain 5 or 6 marks out of 6. The main features of the cartoon are identified and explained, the context is set and recalled information is used to evaluate the cartoon and reach an appropriate conclusion.

EXAM EXAMPLE 13

Now here is a question from special topic 8: The Origins and Development of the Cold War 1945–1985.

> **Explain the significance of this cartoon in the context of events at the time. (6 marks)**
>
> **Use the source and recalled knowledge.**

This cartoon appeared in a British newspaper, September 27, 1948.

Here is a weak answer.

The cartoon is from 1948 during the Cold War. It shows an American looking angry at Stalin's face on a barometer. The cartoon is about problems in Berlin and America looks like it will bomb Russia. The barometer predicts weather and America is worried about that.

Why is this a weak answer?

There is very little scene setting introduction. This answer picks on certain features in the cartoon but fails to develop or explain them. There is almost no recall apart from identifying Stalin and that America and Russia were involved in Cold War confrontation. Uncle Sam as representing America is not identified.

There is also a factual error. America was not about to bomb Russia although the 'superforts' in the cartoon refer to US bombers which were stationed in Britain as a warning to Russia. This answer completely fails to identify that the cartoon is about the Berlin Airlift.

The only explanation of the cartoon is wrong so the answer might only gain 2 out of 6 marks.

How should a good answer be constructed?

Follow these steps to answer any cartoon / illustration question.

1 Check the date. It is September 1948. That should tell you the topic is about the Berlin airlift.

2 Check the source. It is a British newspaper therefore likely to show a biased anti-Russian point of view.

3 Check any characters / figures in the cartoon. The standing figure is Uncle Sam representing the US. Stalin's face is seen on the barometer.

4 Check the words in the cartoon. They are: 'Berlin barometer', 'superforts', and 'stormy, rain, change and sunny'. They are there for a reason – explain the reasons.

5 What other features can you see in the cartoon? The cartoonist has chosen to include these features for a reason. It is your task to explain what they mean and why the cartoonist included them.

A much better answer would be this.

September 1948 was during the Berlin airlift. The crisis had arisen when Stalin had cut all western contact with West Berlin in protest at suggestions by the West for economic reforms of the German zones. The western powers were determined that Russia would not win this contest of power so airlifted all supplies into West Berlin for many months until Stalin admitted defeat and lifted the blockade.

The crisis is represented by the face to face confrontation of Uncle Sam (USA / the West) and Stalin, leader of the USSR.

Stalin's face looks unhappy, possibly at the suggestion of 'change' on the Berlin barometer above his head and the point of his moustache points at 'stormy' suggesting tension between east and west over Berlin.

In response Uncle Sam (USA) stationed B29 bombers ('superforts') in Britain as a warning to Russia that the west would not abandon Berlin. On balance the cartoon illustrates the crisis over Berlin fairly well. It gives the impression of tension and crisis; however by itself the cartoon gives little precise information about the causes of the crisis and indeed is rather biased in its portrayal of Stalin as the 'bad guy'.

Why is this a good answer?

There is a scene setting introduction which contains important detailed recall. The answer not only describes the content of the cartoon but also explains all the features in the cartoon by linking them to the Berlin airlift crisis. Finally there is a direct answer to the question.

This answer would gain 5 out of 6. The main features of the cartoon are identified and explained, the context is set and recalled information is used to evaluate the cartoon and reach an appropriate conclusion. There could perhaps be greater use of detailed recall.

EXAM EXAMPLE 14

Now here is a question from special topic 6: Patterns of Migration: Scotland 1830s–1930s

> **Explain the significance of the illustration in the context of reasons for emigration from Scotland in the later 19th century. (5 marks)**
>
> **Use the source and recalled knowledge. [Q]**

Crofter protests increased in the 1880s and led to violent confrontations

How should a good answer be constructed?

Follow these steps to answer any cartoon / illustration question.

1 Check the date. You have information that suggests this picture relates to the 1880s. Combined with the information accompanying the picture you should know this refers to the Crofter's War, a time when Highlanders fought back against the pressures for change and migration.

2 Check the source. It is a contemporary drawing reporting a struggle between crofters and British marines sent to enforce the law.

3 Check any characters / figures in the cartoon. There are two main groups: civilians are waving sticks, gathering rocks and shouting, and on the other side are armed soldiers / marines. In the middle are policemen who seem to be fighting with the crofters.

A good answer could read like this:

This picture illustrates attempts to evict highland crofters from their homes or persuade them to give up their way of life and leave to find new homes and work elsewhere in Scotland or abroad.

Produced in the 1880s, the picture illustrates part of the 'Crofter's war' when crofters began to resist attempts at forcible eviction. In Skye crofters resisted the forcible evictions as shown in this picture. At the Battle o' the Braes and again at the 'Glendale revolt' crofters fought against marines sent with the police to evict them. Although the marines were armed with guns the crofters fought back with sticks and stones.

The picture relates to reasons for emigration from Scotland because crofters were often forced to move because of hugely increased rents or extra work burdens.

By 1886 a Crofting Act of 1886 gave secure possession of their land to the crofters for the first time and removed one of the main reasons for emigration which was the ability of land owners to evict crofters at will and the desire of highlanders to own and farm their own land.

On the other hand the picture gives a very emotionally biased impression of poor crofters fighting against the government forces supporting the wicked landowners. The reality was often different and the picture gives no information about the other reasons for emigration such as overpopulation, or landlords who tried to help their people, often paying for their passage to America, Canada or Australia.

Why is this a good answer?

This is a different and perhaps more difficult type of picture based question. The context is established and recall is used well to explain the content of the picture. The answer is a clear attempt to tackle the question set.

This is a balanced answer which explains the content of the picture but also provides information to outline the weaknesses of relying only on impressions given by the picture.

This answer would gain 4 or 5 marks out of 5. The main features of the picture are identified and explained, the context is set and recalled information is used to provide a balanced and appropriate conclusion.

What are the essential tips for answering this type of question?

● Don't ignore the illustration. Do use the provenance (who produced it and when and where) to help you explain why it was produced.

● Don't just describe the illustration. Explain the point being made by the producer of the illustration. What thoughts or emotions did the producer want to stir in the people who saw the illustration?

● Finally do what you are asked to do. Link the illustration to the main point of the question by doing the evaluation asked in the question.

ANOTHER EVALUATION TASK – THE OPINION QUESTION

What is an opinion question?

An opinion question is based on a source in which the author makes clear his or her opinion or view about a person or event. You will be asked how far you agree or disagree with the view.

Are these questions similar to the 'how fully' type questions?

Yes, in a way they are. But the difference is that this time you are asked to identify the opinions of the author and argue either in support or against them.

What do opinion questions look like?

There are several ways these questions can be worded but the bottom line is that the source will contain opinions by an author and you will be asked the extent to which you agree with those opinions.

Here is a selection of past questions, all worth 6 marks.

From special topic 2 (The Crusades):

> **How well does the source illustrate the character of Bohemond as a crusading leader?**

From special topic 8 (The Origins and Development of the Cold War 1945–1985):

> **How far do you accept the views in source C on the development of the nuclear arms race? Use the source and your recalled knowledge.**

From special topic 7 (Appeasement and the Road to War, to 1939):

> **How far do you agree with Eden's justification of British policy during the Spanish Civil War?**

EXAM EXAMPLE 15

> **How well does the source illustrate the character of Bohemond as a crusading leader?**

Source D: from the Alexiad by Anna Comnena, written in 1140

For he [Bohemond] was quick, and a man of very dishonest disposition. Although inferior to all the Latins who had crossed over into Asia, he was more malicious and courageous than any of them. But even though he thus excelled all in great cunning, the inconstant character of the Latins was also in him. Truly, the riches which he spurned at first, he now gladly accepted. For when this man of evil design had left his country in which he possessed no wealth at all (under the pretext, indeed, of adoring at the Lord's Sepulchre, but in reality trying to acquire for himself a kingdom), he found himself in need of much money, especially, indeed, if he was to seize the Roman power. In this he followed the advice of his father and, so to speak, was leaving no stone unturned.

Here is a weak answer to the question.

 The source says that Bohemond was greedy and dishonest but also brave. He is called 'evil design' and 'malicious'. The opinion of this person is that Bohemond was only in the crusade for what he could get. This all seems fair comment given what Bohemond was involved in during the crusade.

Why is this a weak answer?

Although relevant opinions of Bohemond are identified in the source there is little analysis of the opinion or any recall used either to support or counter the opinion. There is a very brief evaluation towards the end but it is unsupported.

This would gain no more than 2 marks out of 6, the main weakness being the lack of evaluation which is what the question requires the candidate to do.

Here is a much better answer.

 Bohemond is described as malicious and dishonest but also courageous. Bohemond had little or no wealth in his own country so accepted riches to go on crusade. The source claims Bohemond wanted to gain wealth and power. He was ambitious, even wanting to seize the power of Byzantium if he could.

This opinion of Bohemond seems supported by the facts. Bohemond was in favour of abandoning his oath to Alexius. He was prepared to negotiate with the Muslim Firouz while at the siege of Antioch and Bohemond refused to travel further towards Jerusalem once he gained Antioch and indeed was insistent that the other leaders kept to their oath so that Bohemond could have Antioch if he could capture it. This evidence suggests that the character of Bohemond was well illustrated in the source.

Why is this a good answer?

The source is used well with appropriate information taken from it. There is useful and relevant recall used to support the opinion in the source. The answer ends with an explicit link to the question and a direct answer to the question asked.

EXAM EXAMPLE 16

> How far do you accept the views in source C on the development of the nuclear arms race?
>
> Use the source and your recalled knowledge.

Source C: from J Isaacs and T Downing, The Cold War (1998)

When Nikita Khrushchev stood up to address the delegates of the Twenty Second Communist Party Congress in Moscow, he had something special to tell them . . . He announced that the Soviet Union had just detonated the largest bomb the world had ever seen—equivalent to more than 50 million tons of TNT . . . This heralded a new generation of Soviet superbombs.

Khrushchev told the party members that he hoped 'we are never called upon to explode these bombs over anybody's territory'. Khrushchev neatly summed up the Cold War's nuclear paradox. Each side devoted huge sums to developing weapons it hoped never to use.

Here is quite a good answer.

As leader of the USSR Khrushchev was announcing to the world the power of his country. It had just exploded the world's largest bomb. However Khrushchev also stated that he hoped it would never be used 'over anybody's territory'.

The authors of the source describe Khrushchev's position as a paradox in that both sides in the Cold War raced to build bigger and more expensive bombs but hoping that such bombs would never be used.

This seems to be an accurate opinion on the arms race. Since 1945 weapons had become more destructive. A bombs developed into H bombs. Longer range bombers and then missiles could increase strike range while nuclear submarines and MIRVS could take destruction to the heart of the enemy.

Nuclear weapons could also be seen as a restraining factor as possible sources of conflict flared in Hungary, Berlin, Cuba, Vietnam and Czechoslovakia. No global nuclear conflict grew out of these.

Why is this quite good but not very good?

Points in the source are well identified but the recall used is presented almost as a list of all the candidate knows rather than tying it closely to the question. Out of 6 this answer would gain 4.

EXAM EXAMPLE 17

> **How far do you agree with Eden's justification of British policy during the Spanish Civil War?**

The source is from a speech at Liverpool by Anthony Eden, MP, the Foreign Secretary, 12 April 1937

The policy of non-intervention has limited and bit by bit reduced the flow of foreign intervention in arms and men into Spain. Even more important, the existence of that policy, the knowledge that many governments, despite all discouragement, were working for it, has greatly reduced the risk of a general war. Six months ago I told the House of Commons of my conviction that intervention in Spain was both bad humanity and bad politics. Nothing that has happened since has caused me to modify that judgement; some events have caused me to confirm it.

Here is a good answer.

Eden claims that non intervention 'has limited and bit by bit reduced the flow of foreign intervention in arms and men into Spain and that the policy has greatly reduced the risk of a general war.' Eden seems to be justifying the British policy of non intervention by saying that peace in Europe had been kept and the foreign intervention in Spain had dwindled away. However in reality weapons and resources were pouring into Spain from Germany, Italy and also Russia. The rebel Nationalists were getting a great deal of help while the democratically elected republic was getting very little. In fact the policy of non intervention angered so many people that they volunteered to go to Spain and fight for the Republic as part of the International Brigades. So I do not accept Eden's statement that the flow of arms and men into Spain was reduced as accurate.

On the other hand it was true that as long as British soldiers did not fight in Spain the risk of war escalating was reduced.

Eden then goes on to say intervention would be 'bad humanity and bad politics.'

I do not accept that description. The Republic was the democratically elected government of Spain and as such had the right to buy weapons on the open market but that was denied by the non intervention agreements. Nor was Spanish democracy supported by Britain or France. Instead they tried to avoid confrontation with aggressive fascism which supported Franco.

Maybe by allowing the war to drag on the death and destruction of the civil war was bad humanity but by intervening the war could have increased in size creating more problems for humanity.

Overall Eden's justification of Britain's policy does not sound convincing.

Why is this a good answer?

All relevant points in the source are identified and explained. They are then commented on with relevant and accurate use of recall. There is a clear evaluative and balanced answer provided to the original question.

What are the essential tips for answering this type of question?

- Identify the opinion of the writer and select appropriate quotes to show those opinions.

- Which, if any, of the opinions do you agree with? Use your own recall to defend the opinion.

- Which, if any, of the opinions do you disagree with? Use your own recall to explain why you disagree.

- Reach a decision. Do you or do you not agree with the opinions in the source? Sometimes your answer will contain the word 'partly', sometimes not in this type of question.

- End with a conclusion which answers the precise question set. Go back and read the question again carefully to make sure your conclusion is the best it can be.

THE 8 MARK QUESTION

Whatever special topic you study for the paper 2 exam, one of the five questions will always be worth 8 marks – and just like the other questions in paper 2, the 8 mark question is predictable and if you follow the processes you will be successful.

Is the 8 mark question really difficult?

No. As it is a bigger question in terms of marks and the number of sources used some students think it is harder. Like all the other questions in paper 2, it is a different type of question, that's all. And some other questions in the paper will be worth 6 marks – so 8 isn't that many more!

What will the 8 mark question expect me to do?

You will be asked a question about three sources. You will be told which sources to use in the question. You will be expected to write at least one page of A4 and preferably more. You will be expected to refer to all three sources AND a lot of your own knowledge. The question will always end with 'Refer to the sources and your own knowledge.'

You will be expected to answer the question. That seems obvious but every year candidates think they will pass this question just by describing the sources. They don't pass!

What sort of questions can I expect?

The 8 mark questions usually ask 'big' overview type questions which aim at the heart of the topic. For example, in special topic 7 on Appeasement, the questions with lower marks will ask about specific parts of the course such as the Rhineland remilitarisation, Anschluss, intervention in the Spanish Civil War or the Czechoslovakian crisis. However, the 8 mark question will usually ask about a big theme that runs through the whole topic – such as why Britain followed a policy of appeasement. Other examples of 'big overview' questions have been:

From 'The Crusades':

> **To what extent did developments in crusading during the Third Crusade lead to a decline of the crusading ideal?**

From 'Patterns of migration':

> **How successfully did Irish immigrants assimilate into Scottish society during the period 1830s–1930s?**

From 'The Cold War':

> **'Ideology was the main driving force behind the Cold War'. How far do you agree with this view?**

Can I just use the sources to answer the question?

Some people do just that – but they only get half marks at most. The question itself gives you the clue as to how to answer the question: 'Refer to the sources and your own knowledge.'

Does that mean I must bring in new knowledge not mentioned in the sources?

Yes, but there are different ways to do that. If you use your knowledge to explain, or develop, points in the source then that would count as your own knowledge just as much as entirely new information not connected to anything in the source.

For example, in the Cold War section a question might ask 'For what reasons did the USA pull out of Vietnam in the early 1970s?' One of the sources might state: 'The growth in public protests, draft dodgers and a whole anti war culture of songs and movies turned public opinion in the USA against the war.' You might then develop that source based information by explaining why, and describing how, young Americans avoided conscription and provide examples of anti war song titles or lyrics. That development would be your own knowledge. On the other hand, you might mention information not contained in the three sources at all such as the growing economic cost of the war or international criticism of America as reasons why America pulled out of Vietnam. These points are relevant and are entirely your own knowledge.

Likewise in the Appeasement section the sources might provide a variety of reasons why appeasement was adopted as a policy and all these reasons could be more fully developed by you. However, it would also be relevant to include reasons not mentioned in the sources as part of your overall answer about the reasons behind appeasement.

Will I have used the sources earlier in the exam for other questions?

Yes and no! Usually you will have used two of the three sources for previous questions.

Since you have used two of the three sources before, clearly you will not be asked exactly the same question as before about the source, so you will not score well if you simply repeat the answer you wrote previously. The secret of success lies in using the sources in the different ways required by each question.

How do markers decide how many marks to give to an 8 mark question?

Markers have a mark scheme which lays out roughly how many marks should be given to certain types of answer.

A very good answer

If you USE the sources (by quoting for example) AND develop the sources by explaining the meaning of points in them AND you include your own knowledge AND you end by giving a balanced, thorough answer to the question you will get 7 or 8 marks – depending on the amount of detailed knowledge you include.

A good answer – better than half marks!

If you refer to relevant parts of the sources (for example by quoting) AND you use a limited amount of recall AND you reach a short and basic evaluation of the sources as the question asks, you will at least pass with between 4 or 6 marks. Many people get this band of marks.

A weak answer

You will NOT pass if you only select some relevant evidence from the sources BUT DO NOT try to evaluate the sources or use any recall. You will only get 1, 2 or 3 marks out of 8 depending on how much evidence you select from the sources. In other words, you will not pass just by describing the content of the sources.

Now try a question for yourself and decide – what do you think the answers are worth?

There now follows three examples of 8 mark questions. There is an example from 'The Crusades' special topic, 'The Cold War' and 'Appeasement'.

Use the marking guidance earlier in this chapter. Ask yourself if the answer you have read is weak and deserves to get less than half marks? Or does it deserve to get between 4 and 6 marks? Or does this deserve to get a really good mark?

Decide for yourself then look at the marker decision after the three examples.

EXAM EXAMPLE 18

Special topic 2: The Crusades 1096–1204

> Study the sources below and then answer the question which follows.

Source A: from a history of the First Crusade by the German monk Ekkehard, written c. 1101

After Urban had aroused the spirits of all by the promise of forgiveness to those who undertook the crusade with single-hearted devotion, almost one hundred thousand men were appointed to the immediate service of God. They came from England, Scotland, Ireland, Brittany, Alicia, Gascony, France, Flanders, Lorraine, and from other Christian peoples, whose names I no longer retain. It was truly an army of 'crusaders', for they bore the sign of the cross on their garments as a reminder that they should mortify the flesh, and in the hope that they would in this way triumph over the enemies of the cross of Christ. Thus, through the marvellous working of God's will, all these members of Christ, so different in speech, origin and nationality, were suddenly brought together as one body through their love of Christ.

Source B: from the History of the Franks who captured Jerusalem, by Raymond d'Aguilers, written in 1101

And so, as we said, when our men were in a panic and while they were on the verge of despair, divine mercy was at hand for them . . . Thus, when the city of Antioch had been captured, the Lord, employing His power and kindness, chose a certain poor peasant through whom He comforted us. On that day, after the necessary preparations, twelve men, together with that man who had spoken of the Lance, began to dig . . . And after we had dug from morning to evening, some began to despair of finding the Lance . . . The youth who had spoken of the Lance, however, upon seeing us worn out, disrobed and, taking off his shoes, descended into the pit in his shirt, earnestly entreating us to pray to God to give us His Lance for the comfort and victory of His people. At length, the Lord was minded through the grace of His mercy to show us His Lance. And I, who have written this, kissed it when the point alone had as yet appeared above ground. What great joy then filled the city I cannot describe.

Source D: from the Alexiad by Anna Comnena, written in 1140

For he [Bohemond] was quick, and a man of very dishonest disposition. Although inferior to all the Latins who had crossed over into Asia, he was more malicious and courageous than any of them. But even though he thus excelled all in great cunning, the inconstant character of the Latins was also in him. Truly, the riches which he spurned at first, he now gladly accepted. For when this man of evil design had left his country in which he possessed no wealth at all (under the pretext, indeed, of adoring at the Lord's Sepulchre, but in reality trying to acquire for himself a kingdom), he found himself in need of much money, especially, indeed, if he was to seize the Roman power. In this he followed the advice of his father and, so to speak, was leaving no stone unturned.

Here is your question:

> **How fully do sources A, B and D demonstrate the motives of those who went on crusade?**
>
> **Use sources A, B and D and recalled knowledge. (8 marks)**

Here is an answer to the Crusades question:

There were many reasons why people went on crusade. Source A suggests religious reasons were important. It states 'they were brought together by their love of Christ' and describes 'an army of "crusaders", for they bore the sign of the cross on their garments and in the hope that they would in this way triumph over the enemies of the cross of Christ.'

Source B suggests the crusaders were motivated by religion because when they captured Jerusalem they hoped to find Holy things such as a lance. The crusaders believed in miracles and God's help – it states 'At length, the Lord was minded through the grace of His mercy to show us His Lance'.

Source C describes a different motivation for going on crusade. It describes how Bohemond was 'a man of very dishonest disposition'. He was a 'man of evil design had left his country in which he possessed no wealth at all' and went on crusade hoping to make money.

However there were more motives than just religious reasons and greed. Some knights went on the crusade because of their love of fighting and while on the crusade they could fight without fear of hell. Many Christians believed that the time of Judgement was close, so the promise of forgiveness of sins tempted them to go.

Some ordinary people who went on crusade were bored with their life in Europe. They had suffered several years of bad harvest and the crusade was seen as a way of solving the problem of starvation. Finally some were under peer pressure to go and others wanted to escape debt back home.

So overall the sources do not really cover all the motivations for going on crusade. They only deal with two of them.

EXAM EXAMPLE 19

Special topic 8: The Origins and Development of the Cold War, 1945–1985

Study the sources below and then answer the question which follows.

Source A: from a television address by John F Kennedy, 22 October 1962

This government, as promised, has maintained the closest surveillance of the Soviet military build-up on the island of Cuba. Within the past week unmistakable evidence has established that a series of offensive missile sites is now in preparation on that imprisoned island. The purpose of these bases can be none other than to provide a nuclear strike capability against the Western Hemisphere.

Several of these new missile sites include medium-range ballistic missiles capable of carrying a nuclear warhead for a distance of more than 1,000 miles. Each of these missiles is capable of striking Washington D.C., the Panama Canal, Cape Canaveral, Mexico City, or any other city in the southeastern part of the United States, in Central America, or in the Caribbean area ...

This secret, swift, and extraordinary build-up of Communist missiles ... for the first time outside of Soviet soil – is a deliberately provocative and unjustifiable change in the status quo which cannot be accepted by this country if our courage and our commitments are ever to be trusted again by either friend or foe.

Source C: from M Sheehan, *The Balance of Power* (1996)

The existence of nuclear weapons strongly influenced the ways in which the great powers behaved towards each other. The danger of nuclear war encouraged the two superpowers in particular to treat each other very carefully, treading with great care when their interests came into conflict. It encouraged both sides to explore the possibilities of moderating their competition through the mechanism of arms control, and it encouraged the development of a balance of power system based upon the doctrine of deterrence; one in which the great powers paradoxically amassed huge amounts of military power in the hope that they would never have to use it. The threat to use nuclear weapons represents an ultimate sanction no state could ignore.

Source E: from the Appeal of the Governments of the Five Socialist Countries to the Citizens of the Czechoslovak Socialist Republic, 23 August 1968

Our brothers, Czechs and Slovaks!

In answering the call for assistance addressed to us by Czechoslovak party and state leaders loyal to the cause of socialism, we have instructed our armed forces to give the working class and all the Czechoslovak people the support necessary to defend their socialist gains, which the increasingly persistent encroachments of internal and international enemies have imperilled ...

The counter-revolutionaries are grasping for power. Having seized leading positions in the press, radio and television, the anti socialist forces have defamed and spat upon everything created by the hands of diligent Czechs and Slovaks over 20 years of struggle for socialism ...

The counter-revolutionaries calculated that in the international situation brought about by American aggressive actions and especially by the activation of West Germany's forces, they would succeed in wresting Czechoslovakia from the commonwealth of socialist states. But these hopes are futile. The socialist states possess sufficient might to defend the cause of socialism.

Here is your question:

> **How fully do sources A, C and E illustrate the reasons for tension between the superpowers during the Cold War?**
> **Use sources A, C and E and recalled knowledge. (8 marks)**

Here is an answer to the Cold War question.

The sources illustrate the reasons for tension quite well.

Source A, by the President of the USA, says the building of missile bases in Cuba 'is a deliberately provocative and unjustifiable change in the status quo'. He says America is threatened by missiles 'capable of striking Washington D.C.', the American capital. Kennedy is worried about the 'build-up of Communist missiles . . . for the first time outside of Soviet soil'.

Source C claims 'The existence of nuclear weapons strongly influenced the ways in which the great powers behaved towards each other.' He thinks the 'The danger of nuclear war encouraged the two superpowers in particular to treat each other very carefully' because 'The threat to use nuclear weapons represents an ultimate sanction no state could ignore.'

Source E is set at the time of the Prague Spring when Czechoslovakia looked as if it might break away from the Warsaw Pact. It claims that Czechoslovakia needs protection against 'persistent encroachments of internal and international enemies'. The source also blames the problems on 'American aggressive actions'.

The sources therefore do show reasons for tension quite well with each side blaming the other for being aggressive. The sources also show that the spread of nuclear weapons is a cause of tension.

EXAM EXAMPLE 20

Special topic 7: Appeasement and the Road to War, to 1939

Study the sources below and then answer the question which follows.

Source B: from an article by Richard Cockett in *Modern History Review*, February 1990

All that Chamberlain's appeasement did in practice was to swell Hitler's appetite for territorial annexation. Appeasement did exactly the opposite of what it had been designed to achieve. Arthur Mann of the Yorkshire Post argued quite correctly that by repeatedly surrendering to force, Chamberlain has repeatedly encouraged aggression. Mr Chamberlain's policy has throughout been based on a fatal misunderstanding of the psychology of dictatorship.

Source C: from RJ Overy, *The Origins of the Second World War*, Seminar Studies in History (1987, 1998)

Could the war have been prevented? It is sometimes argued that if Britain and France had been prepared to confront the dictators sooner, even to the extent of fighting for the Rhineland in 1936 or the Sudetenland in 1938, then major war would have been unnecessary. This is to ignore the reality confronting British and French leaders in the 1930s. They were faced with a confusion of different pressures both at home and abroad. As it was they chose to find areas for compromise which did not fatally weaken British or French interests. It was not lack of statesmanship that was at fault, but the basic weakness of the international structure which Britain and France were trying to salvage.

Source D: from *Why England Slept* by JF Kennedy (1940)

People felt that Hitler in 1938 was merely bluffing. People felt that Chamberlain was badly taken in, but I think Chamberlain could not have fought even if he had wanted to. I believe that Chamberlain was sincere that thinking that a great step had been taken towards healing one of Europe's problem areas. Most people in Britain felt, 'It's not worth a war to prevent the Sudeten Germans from going back to Germany'. They failed at that time to see the larger issue, involving the domination of Europe. But although all these factors played a part in the settlement of Munich, I feel that Munich was inevitable on the grounds of lack of armaments alone.

Here is your question:

> **How fully do sources B, C and D help us to understand British policy towards Germany in the late 1930s?**
>
> **Use sources B, C and D and recalled knowledge (8 marks)**

Here is an answer to the Appeasement question.

British policy towards Germany in the late 1930s was mostly aimed at appeasing Hitler but by 1939 that policy had changed.

The sources are partly useful in helping us to understand that policy.

Source B is perhaps the least helpful since it is opposed to appeasement. However it implies some reasons such as Chamberlain's belief that he could understand Hitler and his actions, summed up in the source as 'the psychology of dictatorship'. The source also implies appeasement was meant to reduce Hitler's demands since it says 'All that Appeasement did in practice was to swell Hitler's appetite' which was 'the opposite of what it had been designed to achieve'.

Source C claims that it is necessary to understand 'the reality confronting British and French leaders in the 1930s' so as to understand appeasement. It states that 'different pressures both at home and abroad' were to blame for appeasement but does not go into detail. What the source does blame is 'the basic weakness of the international structure which Britain and France were trying to salvage.' After the League of Nations was seen to be powerless to stop aggression, appeasement was adopted as a way of finding 'areas for compromise' instead of war.

The third source suggests appeasement was a result of politicians misjudging Hitler – 'People felt that Hitler was merely bluffing' – and that public opinion was not prepared to support a warlike policy. Britain was too weak to fight because of 'lack of armaments' and also appeasement may have been the result of failing to see 'the larger issue, involving the domination of Europe.'

Overall the sources help us to understand many of the reasons behind the policy of appeasement. However other reasons were also important such as fear of communism spreading if Hitler was overthrown and Germany weakened.

Britain was also concerned about protecting its empire in the face of threats from Japan and Italy and although Hitler was the main enemy, Britain's resources were too overstretched to deal with conflict on three fronts.

The voting public also had to be considered. Not only did they not want a return to the Great War, they were also afraid of a future war which would devastate cities with gas bombing.

Finally the question asks about British policy in the late 1930s and at no point do the sources deal with the change in British policy which led to Britain declaring war on Germany in September 1939.

So overall the sources only give some reasons why appeasement was adopted and none at all about why that policy changed.

Make your mind up time

What markers thought of the Crusades answer

This is quite a typical answer and follows a certain formulaic style of describing the sources, selecting some quotes and then writing some recall, finishing with an evaluation. And it works! It will pass!

At first, the answer does not look too good. It seems to be just a selection of quotes from the sources with no development or explanation of the points. However, there is the quite a large amount of relevant recall, leading to an appropriate conclusion which answers the question set.

By applying the marking instructions it can be seen that there is relevant evidence from the sources, the main points in the sources are established and recalled knowledge is used to reach an appropriate conclusion. The evaluation is a bit weak but does mention that only two reasons are given in the sources.

On the other hand the answer is a rather mechanical, formulaic style of answer. It does what is necessary to answer the question BUT does not relate the recall to any development of source content. For those reasons a marker will be thinking of 6 marks but probably not 7 out of 8.

What markers thought of the Cold War answer

This answer relies heavily on the sources and uses only very limited recall. However, it does select relevant evidence from the sources, it does have limited recalled knowledge and it does make a very basic evaluation as the question asks. For those reasons it cannot fail – but nor can it get into the high zone. This answer is worth no more than 4 marks, mainly because it does not explain the points from the source and does not consider any other reasons for tension which are implicit in any question that asks 'How fully ...?'

What markers thought of the Appeasement answer

First of all, it starts with an evaluation of the sources in terms of the question asked and sets the scene for the balanced answer which follows. It establishes that British policy was mainly appeasement but the policy changed.

The answer deals with all three sources fully. It uses quotes from all the sources appropriately to support points made in the answer.

This answer also uses recalled knowledge to develop points made in the sources, for example by referring to the League of Nations failures.

Once the sources have been fully dealt with, there is a balanced evaluation which considers other reasons for appeasement not identified in the source. Lots of recalled knowledge is used here.

Finally, the person who wrote this answer looked carefully at the question and saw the reference to British policy in the late 1930s. Since Britain went to war in 1939 clearly the policy of appeasement changed and that makes a good conclusion since the writer has thought about the question.

For all those reasons this answer gets into the full mark zone – maybe 7 but probably 8 marks out of 8.

Are there any final tips about answering the 8 mark question?

Yes – and here are two!

In the section on timing you will see you should allocate about three minutes a mark in paper 2. So that gives you about 24 minutes to think and write this answer (that's 3 minutes x 8 marks for the question.). Even allowing for eight minutes to think and read the sources – and that's a long time – try it – you will still have 16 minutes to write this answer. Since most people can physically write one page of A4 in ten minutes you should aim to write about two pages of your exam booklet for this answer. Give a marker a chance to give you marks. The more you write the better chance you have.

Here is another tip for the Appeasement section. Prepare for the big overview question – possibly about reasons for appeasement (which could also be disguised as a question about British Foreign policy) – by learning a checklist of all those reasons. Write them down on a part of your question paper. Then put a tick beside each one that is dealt with in your three sources, also identifying which source made which point. That way you will use all three sources. When you are finished you will have some unticked ones. These are the ones to develop as your own knowledge. The ticked ones should be explained and linked to the relevant points made in the sources. That way you can't fail to have a full answer with recall and using three sources.

Below is an example from the Appeasement section but the same strategy can work for the other sections. Decide what the main issues are in your special topic and prepare a similar grid.

	in sources	which one
Fear of communism	✔	C
Need to protect the empire and keep it united	☐	☐
Weakness of British armed forces	✔	B
Feelings that Hitler was justified	☐	☐
Feelings that it was France that was provocative	✔	B
Britain had no reliable allies	☐	☐
Fear of a repeat of World War One carnage	✔	A
Fear of new war involving air bombing with gas	✔	A

Conclusion

Now you are ready for your exam. Good luck.

On the other hand, when a famous golfer was told he had been lucky when he holed a long putt, he replied that the more he practised the luckier he got. In other words, you don't need luck. You have worked hard and you know what to expect in the exam. Eat and sleep well before the exam. Allow plenty of time to arrive at the place where you will sit the exam. Avoid arguments before the exam and be as relaxed as you can be.

And finally...

Use time carefully and all will be well.

And what will Higher History gain you? What advantages has the study of history brought you? In the short term you will know a lot of facts about the topics you have learned. You will also gain a respected qualification which will assist your entry to further education or employment.

But in the longer term perhaps you have gained more than you think. You have acquired many transferable skills which is a major strength of Higher History.

In your extended essay you had to use your skills of planning, researching, organising and presenting.

In paper 1 you had to work against the clock to construct an argument based on an issue. To do that you had to use your information to present a clear argument with a beginning a middle and an end – the essential skills for any presentation you will do in your life.

In paper 2 you had to use your skills of analysis and evaluation. Throughout life you will use such skills to arrive at informed decisions.

The facts of history are in the past but the skills you now have equip you for the future.

Glossary

Context – This means the situation that existed when an event happened and that can help explain the event.

Evaluation – In Higher History paper 1 you are asked to evaluate opinions or ideas such as in questions which start, 'How far do you agree ...?' or 'To what extent ...?' In paper 2 the evaluation questions will often ask how useful or how reliable a source is. In all these cases you are asked to reach a judgement based on your knowledge and skill.

Extended essay – It counts for 30 marks out of the course total of 110. You are allowed a plan of 200 words and two hours to write up this essay in exam conditions.

External assessment – These are part of the final exam. Your extended essay, although written in your educational establishment, is sent away and marked by SQA markers. Likewise your Higher exam – paper 1 and paper 2 – are sent off to be marked.

Historiography – Historians research the past by finding and using evidence to support their ideas. Often historians differ over interpretations of past events. Historiography is the study of those differing opinions. By using your knowledge of these differing opinions you will be able to make a more effective debate type answer.

Internal assessment – Assessments carried out within your educational establishment and marked by your teacher / tutor. There are three internal assessments and each must be passed. You will have a chance to revisit the assessment if you fail and if that is not successful you may be allowed a second chance at passing by sitting an entirely different assessment on the same unit.

Issue – Essay titles in Higher History are issue based. That means they present an idea or opinion to you and it is up to you to use your knowledge to argue for or against the idea.

Paper 1 – The first exam paper you will sit as part of your Higher exam. It lasts for 80 minutes and in that time you must write two essays each on a different unit.

Paper 2 – The second exam paper you will sit as part of your Higher exam. It lasts for 85 minutes and in that time you must answer five questions based on sources relevant to your special study.

Primary source – Any source produced around the time of the event described or shown in the source. Primary sources can also include opinions or descriptions written by people who were alive at the time but who produce the source later – such as autobiographies or memoirs based on diaries kept at the time.

Secondary source – A source produced by someone not directly involved in the events they describe and usually many years later. Historians producing secondary sources such as a text book use primary sources and hindsight to form opinions about the past based on the available evidence.

Syllabus – The exact content of your Higher History course is available on the SQA website **http//:www.sqa.org.uk**. The syllabus defines exactly what could be in your final exam. Each year the syllabus is sampled in the exam which means that some topics will be left out.

Word count – Your extended essay plan must be no longer than 200 words. You must state an accurate word count on your plan